D1549000

TAKE MY LIFE, PLEASE!

TAKE MY LIFE, PLEASE!

Henny Youngman
with Neal Karlen

WILLIAM MORROW AND COMPANY, INC.
NEW YORK

It is the policy of William Morrow and Company, Inc., and its imprints and affiliates, recognizing the importance of preserving what has been written, to print the books we publish on acid-free paper, and we exert our best efforts to that end.

Library of Congress Cataloging-in-Publication Data

Youngman, Henny
Take my life please! / by Henny Youngman with Neal Karlen.
p. cm.
ISBN 0-688-07744-7
1. Youngman, Henny. 2. Comedians—United States—Biography.
I. Karlen, Neal. II. Title.
PN2287.Y62A3 1991
792.7'028'092—dc20 91-12196
CIP

Printed in the United States of America

First Edition

1 2 3 4 5 6 7 8 9 10

BOOK DESIGN BY M&M DESIGNS

In memory of Sadie Youngman, my beloved partner for fifty-six years
To my kids, Gary and Marilyn, who never saw me enough, I guess, while I was out hustling—H.Y.

For Meredith, friend—N.K.

TAKE MY LIFE, PLEASE!

CHAPTER ONE

What I Tell the Young Comics at the Friars Club, or, Just Because You're Eighty-six Doesn't Mean You're an *Alter Kocker*

"Don't look back. Somebody might be gaining on you."

I can't remember whether it was Satchel Paige, or my Uncle Morris, who said not looking back was the key to staying young. It doesn't really matter, because I don't think my problem is what's behind me. No, I'm pretty sure that whoever might be gaining on me is, at this very moment, right in front of my eighty-six-year-old face.

Let me explain. I've just finished my usual meal at my usual table at my usual lunchtime place: the Friars Club in midtown Manhattan. I've just overtipped my usual waiter, Steve, whom I call "Statue," because that's how fast he moves.

That done, I am now free to watch the parade of young comics who come to the Friars Club dining room every afternoon to pay their respects to the old comics. Most of the young comics come here looking for wisdom from the sages; most of the old comics come here to tell lies to each other about the good old days, and to complain about their ungrateful grandchildren.

Talking to these hotshots, I get the feeling that things move much faster in show business these days. When I was their age, back in the days when man was learning to walk upright, I was still telling cornball burlesque jokes in places like Pottstown and Peoria. But today, a lot of these kids already seem to have three-picture contracts, four sitcom-development deals, and two stays at the Betty Ford Clinic.

Still, I don't envy them. Most of these young comics, even the really successful ones, look worried. They don't seem to be having a whole lot of fun. What, they all seem to be wondering, are they going to do if their three pictures or four sitcoms fail? What, they all want to know from us old-timers, is the secret to *lasting?*

Now I don't mean to sound like a blowhard. I like a lot of these young comics, I really do. Robin Williams? He's crazy, he's funny. Then there's that guy Richard Belzer, he comes to the Friars Club a lot, almost as much I do. So if it appears that I'm talking down to these kids, it's because I've learned a few things over the years—and not because I'm an *alter kocker.*

Alter kocker. It's an important phrase for everyone over forty to know, no matter what business they're in.

Literally, it's Yiddish for old shi . . . oh, never mind what it literally means. For sixty-six years, I've always worked a clean act.

Anyway, in show business, *alter kocker* means an old guy who was once a player in the industry, but who now sits around telling the same goddam story to whoever will listen about the time he played polo with Sam Goldwyn, Clark Gable, and Gummo Marx.

In life, meanwhile, being an *alter kocker* means that you've closed up shop, put your brain in the closet, decided that you're happier thinking about what happened yesterday than figuring out what's going to happen tomorrow. I've got a joke that goes, "A guy came up to me and said he'd bet me fifty dollars that I was dead. I was afraid to take the bet." That "I" in the joke is an *alter kocker*.

That "I" ain't me. I'm no *alter kocker*. That's why when the kid comics come up to my Friars Club table and say, "Mr. Youngman, how old *are* you?" I don't tell them I'm eighty-six. That's just a number, it doesn't mean anything. Instead, I tell them a joke.

"I'm so old," I say, "that when I order a three-minute egg here, they make me pay up front." They usually laugh, and to me, that means everything. If I can still make someone laugh, then I still must be alive.

And if my lunchtime audience laughs hard enough, I'll tell some more jokes to these hip kids with their skinny black ties and suitcoats with shoulder pads big enough for Bronko Nagurski. A lot of *their* jokes, of course, I don't get. Their jokes are too complicated for my taste.

For me, every good joke is really a simple cartoon—you can *see* it. Let me give you an example. "A man says to another man, 'Can you tell me how to get to Central Park?' The guy says no. 'All right,' says the first, 'I'll mug you here.' "

Here's another simple one: "Two guys are in a gym, and one is putting on a girdle. 'Since when have you been wearing a girdle?' says his friend. 'Since my wife found it in the glove compartment of our car.' "

Do you see what I mean? If a joke is too hard to visualize, I tell the young comics, then what the hell good is it? Personally, I forgot about the sophisticates years ago. I tried smart comedy once, but people wouldn't believe it from a guy like me. I play for the masses. I tell easy jokes where people don't have to think. My jokes happen to everybody. Some people get embarrassed because my jokes are corn. They're plain, but for sixty-six years they've made people laugh. And you got to have a few laughs. If you can't have a few laughs, I tell these worried kids, what good is life?

Meantime, while I'm sermonizing in the Friars Club dining room, all around me the *alter kocker* comedians are finishing their lunches, pulling out cigars, and complaining about their long-dead agents. Right now, two tables down, I can hear a comic who is young enough to be my younger brother telling stories about Walter Winchell and Abbott and Costello. Mind you, I don't have anything against these dear departed. Hell, Walter Winchell was the one who first called me "the King of One-Liners." And I *discovered* Abbott and Costello.

It's just that I prefer to spend my lunchtime working the phone that is at all times on my Friars Club table. The phone's not for show, it's really plugged in. You see, I like to be reachable at all times by agents and bookers, not to mention panicking mothers who have just learned that the ventriloquist they hired for their son's bar mitzvah party has just come down with strep throat.

That's why I keep my name listed in the New York phone book. You've always got to let people know that you're alive, that you're okay, remind them that you're in *business*. Sometimes you don't need the phone to do that—when the William Morris theatrical agency moved its headquarters across the street from my apartment on Fifty-seventh Street, I put a large sign in my window with the words BOOK THY NEIGHBOR.

But, usually, I need Ma Bell's help. I spend about ten grand a year on long-distance, calling up bookers across the country and letting them know I'll be in their area in three months, and have they got anything for me? And when I'm not dialing, I'm waiting for somebody, *anybody,* to call.

And when that anybody calls up my listed phone number, chances are excellent I'll be the one to answer the phone. And if I don't, a real live answering-service voice that sounds like someone's cranky mother-in-law will say, "Henny Youngman, King of the One-Liners," and demand your phone number. And you can bet I'll call back. Not because I'm lonely, but because you never know when a bar mitzvah band has canceled because of a last-minute case of bad vibes.

"Bad vibes." Not bad for an eighty-six-year-old, eh?

Anyway, the point. The point is that this morning I booked myself for two shows a night for a week in Miami from my barber's chair. Then, about forty-five minutes ago, just as Statue was serving me my soup, I got a call from the president of Penn State asking me to come to campus and perform. And who knows who's going to call this afternoon?

So I laugh when young comics in search of trade secrets come up to me and ask college-boy questions like "What is the meaning of comedy" and "What makes a joke funny?"

"So you want to know the secret of success in comedy?" I tell the Young Turks. *"Stay on phones!"* And I mean it. Once, a young comic asked me what comes first when cooking up new material—the punch line or the setup. What comes first, I told him, is the phone call. So if the phone rings, I tell the kid comedians, answer it. It could be a job.

Generally, however, I don't go around giving lots of wise-sounding advice. When it comes to wisdom, I'm usually a believer that those who say don't know, and those who know don't say. Coming up in vaudeville, I learned that comedy is a brutally competitive profession, and there are only so many jobs to go around. Sure you pal around with the guys. But most comics keep their big, important ideas to themselves.

Yes, every once in a while you meet someone like Jack Benny or George Burns, two of the sweetest, nicest men I ever encountered. You even find people like Milton Berle, who threw lots of stand-up jobs my way when I was a down-on-my-luck printer selling business cards for a living on a sidewalk near Broadway. But for every gentleman like these fellows, you usually find five comics who are bastards of the Al Jolson variety.

You didn't know the great Jolson was a bastard of the first order? Let me tell you one of Al's favorite ways of dealing with fellow comedians. Whenever he was in

New York for a run of one of his comedy shows, Jolson would go to a matinee of one of the best vaudeville houses in town. There, he'd scribble down the best joke told by that afternoon's best comic.

Later that night, Jolson would use the joke in his own act. The very next morning, Jolson's lawyer would send over a nasty memo to the unfortunate vaudeville comedian saying that he'd been caught performing a joke that had been written exclusively for Al Jolson. If the comic didn't stop using Jolson's joke, went the letter, his pants would be sued off.

Nice business, huh? True, Jolson was a bit extreme. But, generally, comedians don't go out of their way to help each other. Why? Because *everybody* is competition.

But as the years go by, I find I *do* like to talk to the young guys when they come around. Part of it's because I still remember how several people helped me along the way. And anyway, I don't have any enemies—I've outlived them all. And let's not forget that when you're eighty-six, it's important to keep piling up those brownie points with the Big Guy. So I share with the kid comics.

Stay on phones, I remind them.

"I see," they usually say. "So you answer the phone. Then what?" Then comes Youngman's Second Law of Show Business, which *definitely* came from my Uncle Morris, though I'm sure Satchel Paige would have agreed with the sentiment. Once again, I'm going to have to lay on a little Yiddish. True, Yiddish may not have words for things like microwave ovens or atomic bombs, but it can't be beat for wise sayings. Okay. Are you ready, class?

Nem di Gelt. Get the money.

This piece of advice has many layers of meaning. The

most obvious is, don't believe all the baloney that people tell you when they're describing what they're going to do for you someday soon. *Nem di Gelt.* Get the money.

Some people have a different way of saying this: "Wait until the check is in your hands." Let me tell you, that's not good enough. Back in the thirties, I used to play a club where the owner specialized in giving the comics fifty-dollar checks from an account that always had only forty-seven dollars in it. *Nem di Gelt.* Get the money.

But there's another meaning to this phrase, a humbler idea that young comics should remember when maybe they're temporarily not as hot as they were the week before. Yes, you should get the money—but more than that, you should also get the job.

Let me explain. In show business, you've always got your price—the supposed minimum amount of money that you'll play for. Around a half-century ago, for instance, I calculated that my price was one thousand dollars a week. After all, I was a star, I figured. I had just put in a successful run as the house comic on the Kate Smith Radio Show, and was dickering with several Hollywood producers who wanted to put me in the movies.

Back then, flush with my recent success, I was as cocky as any of these kids coming around the Friars Club with their questions about the meaning of comedy. Anyway, the dickering with Hollywood guys went on and on. And on and on. In the meantime, nobody in New York was meeting my price. I was successful, but I wasn't working.

One night I was sitting in Lindy's restaurant on Broadway *kvetching* and moaning about how rough my luck was. I was sitting at a table with a jeweler named Chuck Green. The reason I was sitting with Chuck was that he was a show-biz buff who was always willing to buy sponge cake and coffee for a performer in the dumps.

Actually, chumming up to us was part business for Chuck—he made a nice living selling diamond pinkie rings to performers headed out on the road. Everybody in vaudeville who had any dough at any given time wanted these rings—and not just because they made a nice flash on stage. The rings, you see, were hedges against disaster—if you went bust touring the provinces, you could always pawn your ring and make train fare back to New York.

My problem, however, was that I was going bust right there in Lindy's. But just as I was hitting the high notes of my personal soap opera, Chuck interrupted me. "You ought to be working somewhere," he said, "instead of sitting around here sponging sponge cake and coffee and bending my ear."

"I'd work," I protested, "but I can't get the money I'm worth."

"You're never worth more than the money you can get," Chuck said. Remember that, students. You're never worth more than the money you can get.

But Chuck wasn't through. "How much are you asking?" he asked. I told him a grand a week, and he spit half his cheesecake across the room. "Who the hell do you think you are, Rin Tin Tin?" he continued. "How long have you been out of work?"

I told him I'd been idle for about ten weeks, which meant I'd lost ten thousand dollars. With that, Chuck spit the other half of his dessert. "Why lowball your value?"

he said. "Why not be out of work for ten weeks at ten thousand dollars a week? Then you'd be able to say you lost a hundred grand. Then you'd really be a player. But if you want to rejoin planet Earth, why don't you figure that what you've lost is three-fifty a week—which is what you might have been making if you didn't have such a swelled head."

I had to admit that he had a point. A couple of weeks later I went to work for—you got it—three hundred and fifty bucks a week at this club Billy Rose owned called the Casa Mañana. Does anybody still remember Billy Rose these days? Kids, go to the video store and rent *Funny Lady*. There's Billy Rose.

Oops, pardon me. Was I sounding like an *alter kocker?* Forgive me. I'm eighty-six for Chrissakes.

Anyway, once again to the point. It's better to swallow your pride and get the money at $350 a week than to be Mr. Big Shot and *not* get the money at $1,000 a week. So when you're working the phone, talk to the people who will be writing the check. Negotiate. Come down a little from your price, if need be. Get the money, but more than that, get the job.

Let me give you an instance of one of the more brilliant examples of someone getting both the job and the money. It happened about fifty years ago, and involved me and a very smart fellow named Irving Lazar. These days Irving is known as Swifty, and he's probably the most important literary agent since Moses delivered the Ten Commandments.

In modern times, Lazar is all pomp and dignity, the guy whose party you want to get invited to the night of the Oscars. Back then, when he was still Irving, he hustled like the rest of us.

But my, he was swift. One night back in the Stone Age, I run into Irving at a party in New York. We start talking, and I mention that my agent, Ted Collins, was taking a 20 percent cut of my salary. When he hears that, Irving gets very, very angry. "That's too much," he says. "He's not entitled to that much. Let me handle the matter, and I'll get him down to fifteen percent."

I was amazed a couple days later when Lazar called me back with the good news that he'd gotten Collins to take a 5 percent cut. I was even more amazed when Irving told me the *other* news—that his fee for handling the matter was 5 percent of my salary. And that's how Swifty Lazar became my agent. He got the job, and he *nemmed* my *gelt!*

"Okay," the polite young comics at the Friars Club generally say at this point, "very nice, Mr. Youngman." But I can usually read their faces. These kids came looking for advice, and what they think they've gotten is comedy's *Fiddler on the Roof,* with my wise Yiddish sayings and my stories of people with names like Kate Smith and Al Jolson.

"Is there anything else we should know?" they ask, as they tap their toes and try to remember what time the limo will be picking them up to take them to the Lear jet that will fly them to Arsenio's couch.

If my phone's not ringing at the moment, I'll leave them with one last piece of advice. It's not just about show business, but about *life* business. Yes, it's in Yiddish, but I promise them, and I promise you, my reader, that it's the last Yiddish proverb I'll throw at you. I'm a comic, for Chrissakes, not a rabbi. But this is a good one, and it's taken me eighty-six years to figure out its truth. Everybody ready?

Mensh tracht, Gott lacht.

Man plans, God laughs.

In other words, life is an accident. Plan ahead as much as you want, plot out your career moves as though it's an arithmetic problem. Fate will usually have something else in mind. It might be great, it might be terrible, but all you can do is hang on.

Take my life, please. It's all been a big mistake. Even at eighty-six, I still don't know what the hell happened. It's been like a dream. Sometimes I wonder what would have happened if I had been a little better student, and had managed to graduate high school. Or what if I'd been a little better violin player, and been able to keep plinking out a living with rinky-dink borscht-belt bands? Or maybe what if I'd been a little better business-card printer, and been able to support my family that way in a manner above the poverty line? I'm not sure, but I do know I wouldn't have had this wonderful life in show business.

Like I said, it was all a mistake. I was an absolute nobody the first time I took my jokes on the radio. After the show, the CBS producer came up to me with a contract to be a regular. The first thing he asked me was, "Where's the rest of your material, and where are your writers?"

I said, "Who? Where? What material?" I was a greenhorn. I came out of left field. I didn't even know enough to copy anybody. I wasn't trained. I wasn't taught. But overnight I became a star, so I had to learn the business.

I got $250 for that first show. When I got home, my mother said, "Since when have you been funny?" I showed her the check—and that's what convinced her I was funny.

Even my most famous joke was an accident. Not long after I got hired to do *The Kate Smith Show,* my wife, Sadie, may she rest in peace, came backstage a few minutes before we went on the air. Sadie brought along some of her friends, and they were all talking and giggling while I was trying to read my script. Showtime was coming, and the noise level was rising from my personal peanut gallery. Finally, I couldn't take it anymore. I took Sadie by the elbow, and brought her over to a stagehand. I wanted him to bring her out to sit with the studio audience.

"Take my wife," I said to the guy. *"Please."*

Thank you, Sadie, for that joke that made my career, and the fifty-seven years of marriage that made my life. Sadie always stood by me; she agreed to marry me at a time when her parents were convinced I was a bum. Later, when I started getting jobs telling jokes at midnight to crowds of gangsters and swells and drunks, she never complained.

Sadie never really knew from show business. Over the years, she learned a few of the ropes to get by, but all her life she was really a simple Jewish girl from Brooklyn. In the early days, she never understood why, after I finished my nightclub act, I always had to head over to Lindy's and schmooze up the columnists like Winchell, Damon Runyon, and Jimmy Cannon until four or five in the morning.

Though Sadie usually had to put our children, Marilyn and Gary, to bed by herself, she never asked me to change—she knew the joke business is what I love to do, and what I had to do. While she was alive, I always called her my million-dollar baby—before taxes.

Now that Sadie's gone, I can tell the story of my life. I ran into a lot of rough characters and strange incidents around vaudeville and nightclubs in my day, and I always tried to shield Sadie from what was going on around me. Not because *I* had anything to hide, mind you. It's just that Sadie was a worrier. If I had told her everything that was going on around me, she wouldn't have slept a second until I returned home from my late-night rounds.

So now she's gone. So now I guess there's nobody I have to protect from the truth. Sigh. I wish there were.

But let me warn you. There will be a number of gangsters in my tale, as well as some tales of shoot-outs and stabbings that went on backstage and in the audience while I was trying to tell a joke and make a buck. Dutch Schultz will pop up (and almost get killed in my presence), as well as such mobsters as Longy Zwillman and Waxey Gordon and Legs Diamond.

Sadie, if you're listening, close your ears—for there will also be bootleggers, hookers, madams, and card-sharps in this story, not to mention a Dallas strip-joint owner I got to know by the name of Jack Ruby. And worst of all, you're even going to hear about lawyers and agents.

But, thankfully, my life story is a happy one. Most of it's on the brighter side of things, where you'll meet stars like Sinatra and Berle and my old childhood chum Jackie Gleason. There will be Vegas and Hollywood and Paris and London. And most of all, I hope, there will be laughter.

Throughout it all, of course, there will be me, Henny Youngman, wondering how the hell it all happened. So, Uncle Morris, pardon me, but for once I'm going to look back. The only thing gaining on me at the moment are my memories. I hope you enjoy them.

CHAPTER TWO

Ancient History, or, I'm Sorry, But My Publisher Insisted

To be perfectly honest, Chapter Two is the place in most celebrity autobiographies where I begin skipping ahead to where I figure the good parts will be. You know, the parts with the broads and the divorces and the gangsters and the famous people doing stuff on their off-hours that maybe you wouldn't expect them to do.

Who actually has time to *read* those Chapter Twos that always seem to begin, "I was born in London in 1905?" Who cares?

I think you know what I mean. After telling us he was born in London in 1905, our celebrity author usually goes right to telling us how destitute he was growing up.

"We wuz poor," he writes, "we ate rocks. We didn't have air. But we didn't know we wuz poor. Because the Shmegegge family was rich with love."

"Baloney!" I yell at this point in these books, as I immediately start paging rapidly ahead. You see, I grew up poor too. And I always knew my family, though rich with love, was poor. I knew this because we never had any money.

Anyway, I was born in London in 1905. I know it doesn't sound right—me, born in London?—but there's nothing I can do about it now. Yet despite what my birth certificate reads, I don't think I quite cut the proper British figure. The Brits have got this certain style, if you know what I mean. Do you know how to tell you're watching a British science-fiction movies? When all the Martians carry umbrellas.

Anyway, because of the way I look and sound, everybody always assumes I'm as Brooklyn as Pee Wee Reese or a Nathan's Coney Island hot dog. (By the way, if any of you readers haven't had a Nathan's Coney Island hot dog, you should. Old man Nathan himself once showed me the correct way to eat his hot dog. First, he instructed, take a little bite to sample the juices. *Then,* and only then, should you put on the mustard and dig in.)

Wait a minute. How the hell did I get in one paragraph from my baby days in London to the correct way to eat a Nathan's hot dog? Am I just wandering in my old age, or is there some connection here?

My grandson Larry, the Method actor, would probably find something meaningful in all this. "Psychologically speaking," he'd say. This, from a kid who used to come to me complaining of headaches, until I reminded him it was *feet* first out of bed in the morning. This, from a kid who still hasn't written a proper thank-you note for the nice pen I sent him when he graduated the New York High School for Performing Meshuggeners. Kids.

Anyway, in my soul of souls, I really *am* Brooklyn. It just took me a couple of years to get there. At the time I was born in London, you see, the Yonkel Youngman family was still in what my other grandson, Arthur, the big-shot psychiatrist, would probably call a period of "transition."

Yonkel, my pa, never knew words like "transition." To him, the constant moving around began simply as a case of keeping his *tochis* out of the frying pan.

In 1893, things weren't looking so good for Yonkel, a dreamy young peasant living in Friedrichstadt, Russia. For one thing, the pogrom-hungry Czar Alexander was actively encouraging his merry bands of Cossacks to gallop through the Jewish shtetls making abundant use of their swords, torches, and swag bags.

It wasn't the czar's pogroms, however, that finally got my father's personal wagon train moving—it was Alexander's draft. Yonkel knew what it meant when he was notified of his impending twenty-year induction into the czar's army: for a Jewish boy, it was a virtual death sentence. If the czar's ill-conceived campaigns didn't get you killed, your Cossack comrades would surely take care of it. Last but not least, Russian Army food was terrible.

My father was an idealist adamantly opposed to physical violence of any kind. Especially when it involved his own anatomy. So instead of visiting the local fixer, he took the second available option. He got the hell out of Russia.

In the shtetl, Pa had been known as a *luftmensh,* which literally means an "air man." He was a sensitive, poetic type, a socialist, a self-taught intellectual who sometimes felt more comfortable living up in the clouds than dealing with the day-to-day problems of getting by in a world where at any second the Cossacks might show up uninvited for dinner. Instead of worrying about the wolves at the door, he pondered the intricacies of opera. Instead of learning an occupation, he preferred to ad-lib.

Not that there's necessarily anything wrong with being a *luftmensh*—such a fellow is as much a Jewish tradition as rabbis with beards. The prototypical *luftmensh* was Leone da Modena, a sixteenth-century Jew from Venice who listed himself as a professional in twenty-six different occupations ranging from *ad hoc* preacher to free-lance epitaph composer. What made him a *luftmensh* was that he knew two dozen trades—but couldn't make a living from any of them.

The author who captured the kind of man my father was was Sholom Aleichem. Look up any of his stories with the recurring character of Menachem Mendel, the luckless but optimistic dreamer, and you've got Pa.

Still, Yonkel Youngman had the good sense to know that there was no future in either the shtetl or the Czar's army. And so, one step ahead of the draft board, the kopeckless Yonkel hightailed it out of Russia and cadged his way to Paris, the most romantic-sounding spot he could think of. Once there, he quickly found what he thought was his dream job. It's easy to see why. As a newly hired member of the opera claque, he could now count himself as a professional applauder.

What, you never heard of the claque? What, you thought stocking an audience with paid clappers started with the press agent who hired teams of bobby-soxers to swoon wherever Frank Sinatra performed? No way. It all began in the early nineteenth century in Paris, with the opera claque.

The way it worked was this. Say a soprano wanted to make sure she got plenty of curtain calls for her performance that night of *Aida*. All she had to do was go to the claque office, and hire as many "fans" as she could afford.

If she wanted the right ripple of tears from the crowd for a death scene, she could rent some *pleureurs*—literally, "rainers." Opera singers could also hire *chatouilleurs,* chatters, who would mingle with the crowds during intermissions and talk up the production. They were the equivalent of the latter-day borscht-belt *tummlers,* those men paid to walk around the Catskills resorts making sure everybody was having a good time, or at least *thinking* they were having a good time. (But more about that later.)

Of course, not all operas are heavy tearjerkers. For happier productions, stars could rent *rieurs*—laughers. My father, meantime, was a *bisseur*. For two francs a night, he would hoot and holler *Bis! Bis! Bis!*" until the singer paying his wages that night was "forced" to come out for another curtain call.

Pa loved opera more than anything else in the world.

He couldn't stand any of the lower forms of show biz, expecially vaudeville. But to a land a job where he was *paid* to hear opera? It was heaven for a *luftmensh*.

Not that Pa was deaf to duty. His own parents fled Russia right around the time he had, setting up their lives in Whitechapel, London's Jewish ghetto. My grandfather was a peasant hatmaker, and in time, he felt he needed his son's help. So Yonkel quit the claque and moved to London.

Briefly. I never learned why Pa left London so quickly and headed for America. Until he had his family, he had a seemingly incurable case of *shpilkes*—ants in the pants. He was always on his way to someplace else. I've always been like that too, for reasons I never understood either. Two weeks straight of one-night stands in places you never heard of? For me, that's always been *living*.

In any case, Pa quickly tired of London and sailed for New York. Upon arrival, he headed immediately for the Lower East Side and the Mills Hotel, the famous haven for just-arrived greenhorns who could afford twenty-five cents a night. He got a job in a sweatshop making caps and hats, went to the vaudeville theater when he could spare the cents, and tried to see clear of the horse crap that covered these American streets that he'd been told were paved with gold.

Happily, Pa quickly found love in the form of Olga Chetkin, a young Russian-Jewish woman who'd recently escaped from Riga with her two brothers and five sisters. Olga and Yonkel married in 1904, and immediately set sail for a honeymoon in London.

The only way I figure Pa got the money for such a hoity-toity honeymoon was from my uncle Morris Kaplan, who was married to Ma's sister Marie. Uncle Morris had dough—a successful businessman, he owned liquor stores and tenements in Brooklyn. It was Uncle Morris who'd paid for the tickets that brought all of the Chetkin sisters over from Riga; he's the only one in the family who I think could have lent money to his brother-in-law.

Whoever gave Ma and Pa the money to go over to London to honeymoon, however, neglected to give them the scratch to get back to New York. It took the newlyweds a year and a half in England to save up the steerage fare back home. Before they had scrounged up enough, however, they had a baby boy named Henry.

That's me.

I only spent the first six months of my life in the Whitechapel neighborhood in London's East Side, so I naturally don't remember much. Yet despite my cameo appearance as a baby in Whitechapel, I think there's a chance that my personal style of bang-bang-bang one-liner comedy originated there.

Let me explain with the example of another Jewish kid from my part of London who ended up doing pretty okay. I'm speaking, of course, of Jackie "Kid" Berg, the onetime welterweight boxing champion of the world whose nickname was "the Whitechapel Whirlwind."

Berg, who was born only a year after I was, got the nickname of "Whirlwind" because of the unusual way he fought. Unusual, that is, for a British fighter. Until the Kid came along, English fighters were famous for being dancers, cutie-pies, guys who would tiptoe around the ring and their opponents as if they were in a china shop.

Berg, who wore trunks emblazoned with a Star of

David and his initials in Hebrew, was a banger. He'd go right into his opponent, throwing punches like a wildman, willing to take punishment in order to give some back. He'd throw more punches in one match than a lot of British fighters could muster in a career. His philosophy was to just wade right in and hit 'em in the guts.

Me too, in my own way. Whereas the Kid threw punches, I threw punch lines. Bam. Bam. Bam. If that didn't work, throw three more. Bam. Bam. Bam. Forget the monologues, the dancing around with clever concepts. Bam. Bam. Bam. And if none of this works, tell them you just got back from a pleasure trip. You took your mother-in-law to the airport. Bam!

Kid Berg and me? It must have been that Whitechapel water.

Ma and Pa's year-and-a-half British honeymoon ended when they finally came up with the scratch to get back to New York with the kid they now called Hen. Once again, I suspect the munificent hand of my Uncle Morris. For the second we landed back in the States, we headed off to Brooklyn and one of the cold-water flats that Morris owned and rented to broke immigrant families like the Youngmans.

For a couple years, the Youngmans reigned as the true wandering Jews of Bay Ridge as we shuttled around the Brooklyn neighborhood to whichever of Uncle Morris's cold-water walk-up apartments was temporarily vacated. Because we were family, he finally gave us a deal on our own apartment—my father only had to pay the rent that the last tenants had paid for the top-floor cold-water flat at 223 Fifty-first Street.

It was an interesting place to have landed—we were the only Jews in a neighborhood composed mostly of Irish families, with a healthy smattering of Norwegians. *"Uff da,"* I remember my Uncle Morris explaining to me in an early lesson of understand-thine-neighbor, was Norwegian for *"Oy vay."*

Now I don't mean to sound like I'm making fun of Morris, because the man was genuinely good to his less fortunate in-laws. It's just that he could be a little tight.

Later in life, when I had made a name and a buck of my own, I used to taunt my Uncle Morris with lines like "You're so cheap that when you go out to eat, the restaurant changes hands three times before you pay the check," and "You're so cheap you send your mother a Mother's Day wire—collect." Morris would laugh, but back when I was a little *pisher,* you didn't joke over money matters with Morris around our household.

Still, it was always an astonishment for me to accompany my Uncle Morris as he shopped for, say, a new suit coat. Shopping was war to him, and in the shops of downtown Brooklyn, Morris was considered the borough's supreme haggler.

Which was no small accomplishment. For among immigrants like ourselves, haggling over price was considered an art form. It wasn't because we were cheap, but rather because we were almost always dirt-poor. Besides, in a time when there were few diversions, haggling could be an entertaining spectator sport. Let me illustrate how it was done back in the days when people knew how to haggle.

Okay, let's pretend we're back at the clothing store with Morris as he searches for a coat. After finding what he wants, Morris would take the coat up front, and the shopkeeper would demand, say, eight dollars.

At this point, Morris would laugh agreeably, and suggest that what the shopkeeper meant to say was *four* dollars.

The storekeeper, starting to get a little indignant, would tell Morris that he meant what he said. He sells clothes as cheaply as anybody, he would reiterate. And anyway, the coat cost him $7.50.

With this, Morris would calmly repeat, "Four dollars." This phase of the negotiation would go on for about ten minutes, with the shopkeeper raging that Morris was out of his mind, and Morris calmly insisting that the shopkeeper meant *four* dollars.

After about fifteen minutes, the merchant would have come down to about $6, and Morris come up to around $4.50. Now, Morris would prepare his best dramatics. Shaking his head and mumbling, he would walk *very* slowly out the door.

Invariably, the shopkeeper would run out the door after him, yelling, "Five and a half!" Morris would turn around, smile, and say, "Five." The two would then shake hands, then maybe go in the back of the store to have a shot of schnapps.

Morris got to so good at the game because he had very deep-felt philosophies about money—feelings that he was constantly trying to pound into my less pragmatic father. Morris's basic idea was that it was better to have money than not. My father got the point. But what Pa never quite understood was how you went about accumulating it.

For hours, my Uncle Morris would lecture his brother-in-law that nothing in the world was more enjoyable than making money. But fun for Jake (he'd left the name Yonkel back at Ellis Island) wasn't counting dollars and cents—it was listening to his collection of eighteen Tetrazzini and Schumann-Heink opera records on his rinky-dink phonograph.

To pay for his collection and to keep the family in coal, Pa found yet one more occupation—sign painter at Kresge's dime store in downtown Brooklyn. By now the *luftmensh* really had to buckle down and work his fanny off; the family had grown to four with the birth of my brother Lester, who came along two years after me.

All in all, it was a pretty typical first act of the Immigrants' American Dream being played out on the top floor of the Bay Ridge tenement. It's easy to ladle on a heavy dose of treacle when remembering events that happened seventy years ago. There's a tendency to forget the bad, gild the good, and come to the old-geezer conclusion that life was so much better in the days before air-conditioning and microwave popcorn. I'll try to stay away from that, try to recall it the way it was.

Times were tough, but we got by. The family, of course, was the glue. My father, being a socialist, wasn't religious in the go-to-shul-every-day-and-rend-your-garments kind of way. Our family went to the synagogue on the High Holidays, kept a Jewish home, and Lester and I were dutifully sent off to Hebrew school to prepare for our bar mitzvahs.

But the real religion Pa taught us was be good to your parents, read books, and listen to opera. Even these simple guidelines, however, weren't quite my style. From my earliest years, I always preferred hanging out on the street with the wise guys to listening to Tetrazzini and eating sponge cake with my folks.

School never held much interest for me either. I was a troublemaker from the first second I stepped into my first class at P.S. 2—I knew I was born to the stage when my first-grade teacher picked up my option after twenty-six weeks. I never figured out why, but I always felt better about myself getting a laugh out of a buddy than an "A" out of a teacher.

But I was never funny at home, because there just didn't seem to be any percentage in it. There was no one in the family whom I felt particularly driven to impress there. My style was to make a quick pass home, go into the kitchen, kiss Ma, wave to Pa, eat my meal, and head back out onto the street. Hence, my mother's famous "Since when were you funny?" question to me after I got my big break on *The Kate Smith Show*. She honestly never knew.

Anyway, Ma was the real comedian in the family. My first memories are of her sitting at the kitchen table trying to learn English with Mrs. Kramer, a dressmaker who lived down the hall. Most of the tutorials quickly degenerated into Yiddish gabfests.

Still, in time Ma caught onto the language enough to rank as the reigning funny Youngman in the apartment. She had a very keen eye for day-to-day nuttiness, and could tell stories like a pro.

Her favorite anecdote came from the one time she served jury duty. An old Jew had taken the stand, and was being sworn in by the bailiff. "Do you swear to tell the truth," the witness was asked, "the whole truth, and nothing but the truth, so help you God?"

"*Nu?*" said the old man, "would I lie to you?"

Not bad, Ma, not bad at all.

CHAPTER THREE

Growing Up in Brooklyn, or, Adolescence—That Period Between Puberty and Adultery

No matter what was going on in the Youngman household, I always found things more entertaining down in the street. My favorite hangout was a block away from our apartment at Mushy Callahan's candy store, where the neighborhood bookies and numbers runners passed their days accompanied by an assortment of guys with cigars surgically attached to their lips.

Sometimes, when my street pals or the candy-store swells weren't around, I'd just wander alone out of my broken-down neighborhood and walk a few miles into some of the finer areas of Brooklyn. Indeed, I could spend an entire afternoon staring up at the rich people's houses in the Shore Road section of town.

I hated them, because I knew I'd never have the chance to live in places like that, with parents who spoke English without an accent, who had dishes that matched, who had the dough to let their kids keep a dog.

There's a joke I used to tell about New York being so crowded that to get over on the other side of the street you have to be born there. Back then, I took the idea of getting over on the other side of the street very seriously—even though I had a sinking feeling that it wasn't meant to be for the wise-guy eight-year-old son of a broke sign painter who knew chapter and verse about Puccini but not a lick about the Brooklyn Dodgers.

Naturally, Pa thought that the best way to salvage his wayward son was with a violin, and not a baseball glove. While I dreamed of being the next Barney "the Yiddish Curver" Pelty, the ace Jewish southpaw of the St. Louis Browns, my father instead saw visions of me taking bows from the orchestra pit of the Metropolitan Opera.

Actually, my father's dream was no different from that of most parents of young Jewish boys back then. For a Jewish boy in Brooklyn, getting a violin was as much a tribal ritual as a *bris* and bar mitzvah.

And so, I was given a violin, courtesy of my aunt Marie, Morris's wife. Pa also went beyond the call of duty, giving me a buck a week to take to Mr. Anthony Di Trinis for my weekly one-hour violin lesson.

That was a lot of dough back then for a sign painter, but Pa kept it up for five years. I think he knew from my first squawk that I'd more likely work for the Metropolitan Transit Authority than the Metropolitan Opera, but he always kept after me, hounding me to practice. Sometimes the noise got to be too much, and he'd send me out my bedroom window, which adjoined the roof of the tailor shop next door.

It's an easy joke, but it's sitting right there. I was probably the first fiddler on the roof.

Sorry about that.

My first real shining moment with the violin came a few years later, when this tough Irish kid came up to me on the street as I walked home from a lesson. If I didn't hand over my fiddle, he told me, he'd beat the sheeny tar out of me.

I don't know what came over me—I'm not an especially brave man. Probably, it was just knowing that whatever this kid might give me, it wouldn't be near what I'd have to live with if I came home without my violin.

So, as the kid reached for the case, I took a wild roundhouse punch at him. Somehow the punch landed lucky, and the Irish kid went down minus a couple of teeth.

The news of my first-round KO went around the neighborhood faster than you could say "freak of physics." Youngman, went the word, is a fighter!

Emboldened by my success and newfound status, I briefly dreamed of a career in the ring like that of such Jewish tough-guys as Kid Berg, Kingfish Levinsky, Kid Kaplan, or Joe "Yussel the Muscle" Jacobs. I sparred around the neighborhood, and finally volunteered for a peewee fight down at Shansky's Gym, a subway ride away.

I still remember the bell. I still remember waking up with my second, Geoff Pollock, fanning a towel over my face. I still remember his girlfriend Sharon saying, "Oh my! Oh my!"

My new nickname in the neighborhood was One-Punch Youngman, as in one punch and out. It helped save my good name among my buddies, of course, that *I* was the one who coined the nickname, as soon as I came to. It was a funny line, the guys all laughed, and I knew I still belonged.

In ethnically mixed working-class neighborhoods like ours, you see, you had three choices when confronted by tough guys who didn't approve of the length of your nose or the day of your Sabbath. You could fight—which I now knew was not my calling in life. Or you could run—which meant hiding out in shame in your parents' cold-water flat until you were old enough to move away from the neighborhood.

Or you could crack a joke, make your tormentor put down his fists and laugh. Hence, One-Punch Youngman. What a card, the guys all laughed as they took me back to the neighborhood, my reputation as a swell intact.

My only real competition for the title of champion neighborhood cutup was this Irish kid who lived a couple of blocks down. This kid had it rough growing up; his father abandoned the family when the boy was eight, and his mother had to go to work as a token clerk down in the subway to support the brood.

But young Jackie Gleason never let on if he was hurting inside—and he was as damn funny then as he was later in life. We grew up together, came up in vaudeville at the same time, and stayed close forever. I still miss the Great One.

Having Jackie around, of course, made me work harder at generating the laughs. In time, joking around, always being ready with a sharp line, got me in good with the bookies and characters with pinkie rings who hung around the candy store.

As long as they knew you showed respect, they loved to get the needle. "Is your family happy? Or do you go home at night?" I'd say, or, "It's good to see you. That means you're not behind my back."

Not great stuff, but good enough that the older guys let me hang around and run errands for them for an occasional dime or quarter. I liked the attention, but I didn't have a lot of illusions as to the characters of some of these candy-store wiseguys.

A few of the older guys I'd joke around with in the store called themselves "the Rowing Club," because they had a big rowboat that they kept tied up to one of the docks alongside the East River. Once in a while they used to take me out for a ride; some other times I'd go out to the docks and they'd tell me to scram in no uncertain terms.

Whenever that happened, I'd just sit and watch as the club members rowed out to a freighter parked in the harbor, then took on board a few large canvas bags. One day, I saw them being chased into shore by a police boat. As the cops neared, my wiseguys dumped the large bags overboard. I figured the abandoned booty was bootleg booze—no big deal.

A couple weeks later, however, I saw the pictures of several Rowing Club members on the front page of the *Brooklyn Eagle*. It wasn't hooch those guys had been smuggling in those canvas bags—it had been illegal Chinese immigrants.

Apparently, if members of the Rowing Club ever got cornered, they simply dumped the living evidence overboard. I felt sick for a month after reading that story and realizing what I'd seen. Remember that, next time you read a Damon Runyon story about how romantic these tough guys were.

Not that I myself was any Goody Two-Shoes. School, as I've said, was not a high priority. To this day, I'm still not sure how they ever let me out of P.S. 2. My patter there was the same as at the candy store, but what I took home from class wasn't dimes but letters from teachers warning Pa of his curious son Hen's dire future.

Still, I ignored Pa's pleas to hit the books. Who had time to study, what with violin lessons, hanging out, and Hebrew school?

To my parents, the only thing worse than me not being able to graduate high school (which I never did) would have been me not completing the studies necessary to have a bar mitzvah.

In this day and age, when the ceremony has taken on the glitz and glamour of a competitive event, it's hard to imagine how simple our little bar mitzvahs were back then. All you needed was a rabbi, a *minyan* of ten Jews, and a trembling thirteen-year-old who'd memorized a few prayers.

The rabbi chanted a little, the boy chanted a little, everyone slurped down a shot of schnapps and bit into a *kichel* or a piece of herring, then everyone went home. It was no big deal. Today I am a Man. Tomorrow I'm still a thirteen-year-old *yutz* who has to take violin lessons.

In modern times, of course, the emphasis is often more on the bar than the mitzvah. Not that I'm complaining, mind you—the new style of expensive bar mitzvah has been very, very good to me. What I still get paid to perform at one would have kept my broken-down shul in Bay Ridge in *kichel* and herring for the entire Roaring Twenties.

Still, you can't help but wonder about some of today's grandiose affairs. Let me tell you a true story. A few years ago, I had just finished performing at a bar mitzvah out on Long Island, and headed over to the buffet.

Over the table was a life-size sculpture of the bar-mitzvah boy rendered in ice. As I ladled fruit salad onto my plate, I heard two women behind me commenting on the sculpture.

"It's beautiful," said the first woman.

"It's a perfect likeness," agreed the second woman. "Who did it? Epstein?"

"Don't be silly. Epstein only works in chopped liver."

My own bar mitzvah had to be postponed sixty years from its original date. The morning before the original big date, you see, my Uncle Velvl died. The ceremony was called off—and it wasn't until over half a century later that I finally got to say, "Today I Am a Man." But you'll have to wait for that story.

I don't recall being too torn up by missing out on my big day. No, when I think back to those days, what I most remember is the entire Youngman family heading out to Coney Island on the farthest finger of Brooklyn. Back then, a Saturday afternoon trip to Coney Island was an every-summer-weekend ritual for seemingly every poor family in New York looking to escape the city heat.

They began arriving at Coney with the first crack of light; a mass of working-class Greeks, Jews, Italians, blacks, Irish, Poles, Germans, and every other known nationality crowding onto the beach. It wasn't exactly the brotherhood of man, but everybody got along pretty well.

Over seventy years later, I can still recall the details of a weekend at Coney Island as if it happened yesterday. (Strangely, at my age, it's sometimes harder to recall what really *did* happen yesterday.)

Like everybody else, our Coney Island–bound family would get off at the Stillwell Avenue subway exit, and walk south toward the boardwalk, bathhouses, and beach. Some of the bathhouses were like fancy athletic clubs, complete with swimming pools and expensive restaurants.

Our family used the teeny dressing rooms that people set up in their backyards. Sometimes, when Pa was feeling flush, he'd treat the family to the Municipal Baths on Surf Avenue and Fifth Street, where you could rent a locker for a dime.

The only thing I can compare to the crush of people on the Coney Island beach is the subway at rush hour. Every hundred-yard stretch of sand held scores of kids making sand castles, young lovebirds smooching, and college kids preening and doing gymnastics over the supine bodies of suntanning *bubbes* of every race.

In this setting, eating was quite an adventure. Have you ever tried to have a picnic in a subway car at rush hour? Ma wouldn't allow us to eat the food sold on the boardwalk—not while she was around would a Youngman child be allowed to chase down the aromas that drifted to the beach of frying hot dogs, cotton candy, corn on the cob, or even the knishes. "Dreck!" she'd mutter as she unloaded the thermos bottles and brown bags of food from the suitcase filled with bathing suits and spare clothing that Pa had lugged from home.

When dusk came, Ma, Pa, and Lester would get back on the subway and head home. I'd wander up to the boardwalk, and meet up with my buddies who had also finally managed to shed their families. Among my rogues' gallery of pals was Art "Thumbs" Simon, the thumb-wrestling champ of Bay Ridge; Chaz "Twinkletoes" Strouse, whose mother made him take dancing lessons, and Craig "Lefty" Hunegs, whose name I could never figure out, because he was right-handed.

Any available money was immediately pooled for the benefit of all in that day's gang. Finally, after a day of waiting with our families, we could all taste the cotton candy and play the Skee-Ball that had been denied us.

From the boardwalk, we'd stroll on the Bowery, between Surf Avenue and the boardwalk. Past Feltman's Beer Garden, we'd loiter and count our pennies to see if we could get into the freak show or the "Chamber of Horrors" waxworks. We'd hang outside the jazz halls and listen to the music, or head over to the rides—the Cyclone, the Loop-o-Plane, the Dodgem Speedway.

The gang would convene until midnight, when Coney Island shut down. Then we'd all stumble back on the subway, headed for our tenement homes and our slumbering immigrant families.

Another favorite summer activity was an outing to see the Dodgers at Ebbets Field. No one could ever afford a ticket, of course, but several times a season the Bums would have a promotion where for two Wheaties box tops kids could get into the game for free and sit in the nosebleed section. There we'd all sit with our brown bags filled with sandwiches, supplemented by a nickel soda.

What I always wanted to see at the ballpark more than anything else was for a Dodger to hit the Abe Stark sign on the right-field wall. Stark, besides being the Brooklyn borough president at the time, also owned a clothing store. He put up an advertisement at Ebbets Field that said, HIT THIS SIGN. WIN A SUIT.

The problem was that a player had to hit the sign—which was right on the ground—on the fly. A guy would have to hit a four-hundred-foot line drive that was two feet off the grass to hit it. I never saw it happen—Abe Stark was no dope.

What I *did* witness at Ebbets Fields, however, was one of the most astonishing bits of comedy I've ever seen in my life. You truly had to be there to understand how funny it was, but the event has gone down in baseball history.

In 1918, Casey Stengel was still decades away from being the goofball wizened ancient who managed the Yankees to so many pennants. Back then, he was just a goofball outfielder coming to the end of a not-bad playing career.

Anyway, the fateful event occurred on one of those Ebbets Field knothole gang days when our entire Bay Ridge contingent of street kids was in attendance in the stadium hinterlands. Right around the fourth inning, Gleason noticed a sparrow fly right into the bullpen wall not too many yards away from us. Playing the outfield, Casey Stengel noticed too. At the end of the inning, he walked over to the dazed bird, cradled it in his hands, and headed back to the dugout.

When Casey returned to the field an inning later, he offered a deep bow to fans in all directions. No one knew what was going on, but all eyes were on the well-known daffy outfielder. After his final bow, Casey doffed his cap, and the by-now alert sparrow flew from his head and into the eternity of all-time great gags.

I can't emphasize enough how much that event impressed me. While nobody can remember anybody else on that 1918 Brooklyn Dodgers team, Casey's joke has taken on a life of its own. It was pure and simple shtick, an easy tag by which he could always be remembered. It was a lesson I never forgot.

There's a flip side to this lesson, however, that all would-be comics would be wise to study. Almost half a century after the sparrow incident, a stooped-over Casey appeared at a Dodgers Old-Timers Game in Los Angeles. I was in town shooting an episode of *Rowan and Martin's Laugh-In,* and thought it might be fun to head out to Chavez Ravine to see some of my old buddies from the Brooklyn days.

Anyway, some Dodger PR man convinced Casey to reprise his famous old bird trick. They got a sparrow from an L.A. pet shop, dazed it by spinning the bird around by its tail, then put it under Casey's hat. Casey dutifully went out to greet the crowd, and doffed his cap. The bird, still unconscious from its twirling, fell to the ground like a rock.

The gag was a bomb. And the lesson was obvious: You can't force your shtick. If it doesn't happen naturally, if it looks forced, or too preplanned, then the magic is gone—and you'll sink faster than Casey's nauseous bird.

Yes, I've got some fond memories of my boyhood in Brooklyn. But my favorite memory doesn't involve baseball players, gangsters, candy-store wiseguys, or wise and ancient rabbis. Rather, it's an event that took place on the tenement roof of plain old Izzy Feinstein, one of my father's band of culture-loving immigrant friends.

Izzy was even more of a dreamer than Pa. By day, he worked his ass off in a sweatshop making brassieres. By night, the shy and slight, balding man was heckled nonstop by an unbelievably domineering wife, whose voice, I kid you not, could carry for three blocks. Izzy's only respite from the hardships of life came from his books, which were stored in as many battered cardboard boxes as his wife would allow in the apartment.

As far as I could tell, Izzy had only one peculiarity—a firmly held belief that most of the great writers of history were secretly Jewish. I always thought it was hilarious when he tried to foist books on me by his favorite "Jewish" writers. "Hen," he'd say, "here's *Richard III,* by Velvl Shakespeare."

Izzy and Pa loved talking over the arts, and on hot summer nights, our entire family would sometimes head over to the roof of Feinstein's tenement. Up there we would find most of the building's residents, all attempting to escape the stifling heat and rampaging roaches of their unventilated Brooklyn-in-August apartments.

It was a party scene that was replayed on working-class rooftops all over New York. While the parents argued politics and gossiped, the younger tenants looked for possible dates. We kids, meantime, would roll out blankets and pillows and lie down on the tar. We'd stare up at the stars, and talk about how one day we were going to get the hell out of Brooklyn and see the world. Often, our parents allowed us to sleep on the roof or the fire escape all night.

One midnight Saturday on Izzy's roof, I was interrupted in the middle of a heated debate with my cousin Jimmy Kaplan concerning whether Shoeless Joe Jackson was a better hitter than Ty Cobb. What shut me up was a beautiful soprano voice singing what Pa later told me was an aria from *Carmen.*

Everyone who was asleep on the roof woke up; everyone who was talking quieted down. When the aria ended, the crowd wildly applauded this voice that made you want to just sit down and cry.

The singer, it turned out, was a stranger who'd come from Detroit to visit her relatives in the tenement. She was twenty-five, a blond music student, and among the most beautiful women I'd ever seen. Urged on by the astounded immigrants on the roof, she began singing again. Popular songs, opera, burlesque, she knew everything. Even the cars below seemed to stop honking.

Meek Izzy Feinstein, sitting on a blanket a few feet from me, was beside himself with awe. His mouth gaped open and tears streamed down his face as he listened to the singer's vast repertoire. After she finished an Italian number, Izzy hustled downstairs, returning ten minutes later with a box wrapped carefully in brown paper.

The singer was resting when Izzy came back to the roof. Izzy, famous for his shyness, boldly took her hand, gave her the package, and breathlessly told her that she had the most beautiful voice and face he had ever heard or seen. "Open it! Open it!" all the wise guys on the roof yelled.

The singer carefully unwrapped the package. Then, she pulled out two brassieres—the fruit of Feinstein's drudgery at the sweatshop. The young girl thanked Izzy graciously for his generosity, while everyone on the roof laughed and whistled.

Someone must have ratted Izzy out, for five minutes later Mrs. Feinstein came storming onto the roof like Refrigerator Perry. She grabbed the gift bras from the singer, grabbed Izzy by the ear, and dragged him downstairs with the words "You no good bum! A man your age giving such presents to single women!"

I didn't get very much sleep that night on the roof, as Mrs. Feinstein's screamings two floors down penetrated all manner of wood and tar. Finally, around six in the morning, I heard a door slam, and went over to the fire escape to see what was going on.

Down below, I saw Izzy hurrying out of the tenement with a large suitcase. I'd never seen him look so confident or strong as he hustled toward the subway. A few seconds later came the heavyset figure of Mrs. Feinstein. Armed with a rolling pin, she chased after her husband, yelling, "Come back, you bum!"

Izzy came back in time for that night's supper. But to the sweatshop laborers who shared his tenement, Izzy Feinstein never seemed meek again.

CHAPTER FOUR

Starting Off in the Orchestra Pit, or, How I Didn't Know My Brass from My Oboe

Back in the old neighborhood, there was one other diversion as popular as baseball, Coney Island, and rooftop slumber parties—the movies. Luckily, Uncle Morris had bought a run-down theater near our apartment in Bay Ridge, meaning I (as well as all the friends I was able to sneak in through the exit door) could get in free.

In exchange for this privilege, Morris put me to work bicycling reels of whatever movie he was showing to another nearby theater. In those days, you see, movie distributors would try to save money by booking the same picture in two close-by venues, and make the theaters share the one print.

So, while Uncle Morris's place was showing the last two reels of some Pola Negri movie, I'd be racing the first two reels over to the other theater. I'd do this all day, racing back and forth with the same copy of one film.

One rainy day, however, as I was racing back to Morris's theater with another two reels, I almost got hit by a skidding *Brooklyn Eagle* delivery truck. I landed on my ass, and *West of the Peco Mesa* ended up unreeled all over a soggy Prospect Avenue. By the time I rewound the movie and got back to the theater, the audience had been sitting in the dark for half an hour waiting for the next reel.

Surprisingly, Uncle Morris didn't fire me. Failing upward, I was promoted into the theater orchestra. Sitting in the pit under the stage with my fiddle, I was to play appropriate mood music for whatever silent action was going on up on the screen. Besides me, the "orchestra" consisted entirely of one elderly woman tinkling away at a battered, horrifically out-of-tune upright piano.

Anyway, my assignment probably wasn't even a promotion—my pay remained zero. But it was my first real experience playing in front of a crowd, and I liked it. I was even worse at the violin than my partner was at the piano, but it still felt like show business.

The hard part of the job was finding something to play that corresponded to the movie scenario. Since both our repertoires were severely limited, the elderly woman and I came up with some simple rules. If we saw a romantic scene, we played soft. If we saw an action scene, we played loud. If a baby appeared onscreen, we'd play Brahms's "Lullaby."

In spite of my new exalted position in the pit, I

couldn't stop goofing around. Uncle Morris finally fired me for good when he wandered into the theater one afternoon while a Percy Marmont picture was playing. At the moment Morris walked in, Percy was making passionate love to his onscreen lady. The pianist was playing something that sounded like a combination of Chopin and a cat being strangled. I, meantime, was scratching out "There'll Be a Hot Time in the Old Town Tonight."

"Out!" shouted Morris. "Outta my theater! You're fired! And don't ask for a week's pay either!"

"But, Uncle Morris, you don't pay me *any* salary," I reminded him.

This took him aback. A second.

"Outta my theater!" he yelled. And I went.

And so began my career—fired by a relative from a nonpaying job that to be honest I wasn't so good at anyway. Ach, show business.

The answer for a sensible boy, of course, would have been to give up these notions of being a star at something, *anything,* and to get on with the business of growing up into a respectable wage slave living a life of quiet desperation.

But no one has ever accused me of being sensible—in many ways I've always been more of a *luftmensh* than my father. No, my answer wasn't to dedicate myself to becoming a normal citizen.

My answer was to start getting better material.

My Uncle Morris wasn't the first person to forcefully ask me to be so good as to get the hell out of his sight. Indeed, a regiment's worth of my public-school teachers had long before realized that the only way to deal with my nonstop wisecracking and refusal to crack a book was to send me out in the hall.

Perhaps the incident I remember best took place in the classroom of Goldfarb, my social-studies teacher at Manual Training High School. Goldfarb had the look and attitude of Wally Cox playing Mr. Peepers—perfect fodder for an obnoxious adolescent such as myself.

One of the worst-kept secrets at Manual was that Goldfarb had a crush on Miss Charlotte Greenfield, the pretty young English teacher who taught two classrooms down. One day while Goldfarb was lecturing us on something like why Miles Standish and Pocahontas didn't have corned beef and herring on the first Thanksgiving, Miss Greenfield passed by our open door.

Goldfarb, never known for emotional displays, boldly excused himself from our class with the apology that he had urgent business to discuss with his collegue from two doors down. Scurrying into the hall, he intercepted Miss Greenfield and no doubt began an urgent discussion of the finer points of secondary education.

When I saw that Goldfarb was safely out of the classroom, I excused myself from my seat in the back and went up to the front of the room. There, I began a comic rendition of Goldfarb trying to woo Miss Greenfield. I played both parts, and, shall we say, employed certain *exaggerations* in my portrayal.

The class was screaming with laughter, and I kept going. I couldn't stop, not even when I saw that Goldfarb was standing in the back of the classroom, his arms folded, his face as red as horseradish, a vein popping out of his forehead. I couldn't stop because I needed the laughter of my friends more than I feared the wrath of Goldfarb.

After I finished my shtick, Goldfarb slowly walked to the front of the room, where I was collecting the huzzahs of the crowd. As he came closer, Goldfarb seemed more like Mr. T than Mr. Peepers. He grabbed me by my shirt collar, hoisted me off the ground, and shook me for thirty seconds, my toes dangling in air. All he kept repeating was, "You think you're funny? I don't think you're funny."

Goldfarb finally put me down, and directed me for the umpteenth time that year to immediately report to the detention room in the school's basement. I trudged out of the room, accompanied by the cheers of the class wisenheimers. It was like those old gangster movies, when the death-row inmates applaud a condemned man as he takes the longest walk.

I don't know what possessed me that day, but when I got to the basement, I walked right past the detention room. Manual High had always operated on the honor system, so no authority figure was assigned to make sure that kids who'd been kicked out of class actually showed up for their penance. In those days, nobody questioned school authorities; it had certainly never dawned on me before not to report to detention.

But it did the day of the famous Goldfarb incident. I just kept walking past the penal room, pushed out the double doors of Manual High, and walked into an afternoon of freedom. Blinking in the sunlight, I considered my options—and went right to the nearby Fox Theatre to catch a full slate of weekday vaudeville acts.

There were three other vaudeville theaters in the

neighborhood—the Flatbush, the Prospect, and the Orpheum. Every time I deservedly got kicked out of class in the coming years—which, to put it mildly, was a bit *frequently*—I'd simply head out the school door to the magic darkness of these Brooklyn theaters.

I liked just about everything about vaudeville's strange conglomeration of singers, dancers, dog acts, and acrobats. But what I always liked best of all were the comedians.

A full afternoon's entertainment cost fifteen cents at the vaudeville theaters. It was a pricey sum for a kid of my age and circumstances, but I willingly poured every nickel I could grab into burlesque tickets.

I had ways to make the necessary money—I'd been working ever since I was a kid running errands for the wise guys at the candy store. At various times I was also a pin boy at two local bowling alleys, a rack boy at a pool hall, and a water boy at construction sites.

For quick cash, I'd play my violin on the Staten Island ferry. My routine was to try to look like a lovable street urchin, Oliver Twist by way of Bay Ridge. After playing, I'd pass the hat among the ferry passengers, who donated more out of pity for my obvious orphanhood than for my classical-music ability. Afterwards, I'd split my take with the ferryboat captain, and everyone went happily on their way.

And so, I was usually able to scrape together enough swag to get into the vaudeville theaters. What I got for my fifteen cents was a seat in the back, and for me, a look into a world of wonder.

Everybody, of course, knows about vaudeville. Or has at least heard about it. But not very many people, it seems, actually understand how vaudeville *worked.* It wasn't brain surgery, but there was a kind of science to it.

Let me explain. Most vaudeville shows had eight acts, one intermission, and a closer. Using that formula, vaudeville bookers had to jockey and jigger the acts and their positions on the bill to make sure that the audience stayed in the theater.

The first act on the bill was usually reserved for what was called a "dumb" act. It might be a dancing act, or a good animal act that wouldn't be ruined by the commotion caused by late theater arrivals getting seated. The key thing was to have an act that didn't depend on its words being heard.

The second act was supposed to be more entertaining than the first. It could be almost anything, but was frequently a good man-and-woman singing team. The point was to "settle" the audience and prepare it for the show.

Number three was supposed to wake up the audience, and start the show cooking on a slow boil towards its climax. Usually, it was a comedy dramatic sketch that featured a big laugh right before the curtain dropped to signal its end.

Number four had to be better still; bookers usually liked to have an act in this spot that could provide what they used to call the first big "punch" of the show.

Number five was the last act before intermission, and was usually a big act with a big name. This act had to be as big a hit as any on the bill—the point was to give the audience something interesting to talk over during intermission. For that reason, one of the very best acts was always chosen to crown the first half of the show.

The toughest position to fill on the bill was number

six, the first act after intermission. That was because the act couldn't be a letdown from what had come before; at the same time, it couldn't be any stronger than any of the acts to follow. Oftentimes this would be a famous "dumb" comedy act, once again making it possible for the entire audience to get back to its seats without a big interruption of what was going on up on the stage.

Number seven of the show, and the second act after intermission, was usually a full stage act that featured another big name. It generally was a comic playlet, though sometimes it was a serious dramatic playlet if the star was a well-known actor or actress. But whatever number seven was, it had to build audience interest for what was called the "big" act.

This was usually the comedy hit of the show, which was always placed in position eight, right next to the closing act. Generally, this was the act that most of the audience had been waiting for. Almost always, act eight was a comic flying solo.

Booking the show's closer was a little tricky. Much of the audience, you see, would get up to leave the theater after seeing the featured eighth act. So, to try to keep people in their seats, vaudeville bookers had to go for what used to be called a "flash" act.

Once again, it had to be a glitzy performance that didn't depend on being heard perfectly. Usually, bookers went for sight acts—animals, acrobats, or a troupe of Japanese dancing in bright-colored kimonos.

I, needless to say, was usually gone from the theater the second the number-eight comedian took his final bow. In time, these featured comics—who've almost all been forgotten now—replaced Kingfish Levinsky and the Yiddish Curver Pelty as my adolescent heroes.

Ah, vaudeville. Once in a while, someone these days might mention Eddie Cantor, who, decades before he became a huge movie star, reigned as one of the greatest Brooklyn vaudeville comics ever.

But what about those other greats? Does anybody out there still remember the late, great careers of Willie and Eugene Howard, Ted Healy, Lew Hearns, Pat Rooney, Frank Tinney, and Joe Laurie, Jr.? Boy, I wouldn't trade one of those guys for ten Sam Kinisons.

Granted, the material back then was, well, rather primitive. Many comics relied completely on elaborate costumes and ridiculous props. Other spent their entire lives doing slapstick so broad that the Three Stooges would have to be considered reserved in comparison. Some of these gag men did skits, others did stand-up, several more worked in dialects.

Looking back from today, you almost can't believe these dialect comics actually were allowed to perform. Believe me, you haven't seen racism or anti-Semitism until you've seen it performed by a comic wearing blackface or a prop nose. And yet these guys were among the most popular of all vaudeville performers.

Not that I'm taking any moral high ground here; like the rest of Brooklyn, I laughed at the dialect guys. But my real favorites were the comics who just got up there and told straight jokes. These guys I *respected.*

And started to steal from. I can't remember on which of those dozens of days spent hiding from the truant officers in the safety of a vaudeville theater I began scribbling down jokes I'd just heard. But it was a day that almost all comics have had growing up—the day that they were hooked.

After a show, I'd memorize the best jokes from my crib sheet while walking home. After those days at the theater, I'd sometimes go up to the apartment and kiss Ma and Pa hello. Other times I'd go straight to the candy store, and start laying out my newly swiped gags for the assembled tough guys.

Soon I almost had enough jokes for a routine. Not that I was turning into a comedian or anything. For starters, my father wouldn't allow it. For enders, it just wasn't what first-generation Jewish boys grew up to be. A tailor, maybe. A job with the city, if you're lucky.

But a comedian? From this you make a living?

CHAPTER FIVE

A Star Is Born, or, I Still Remember My First Words in the Theater: "Peanuts! Popcorn!"

And still I practiced that damn fiddle. Not that my devotion to the instrument stemmed from any drive on my part to become the next Heifetz. Rather, I simply couldn't resist my mother's pleas to begin acting like a prince and to start practicing, like all the other nice poor Jewish boys sawing away at their violins all over Brooklyn. Okay, Ma, I thought to myself, for once in my life, I'll throw you a bone.

And so, I practice. Sometimes.

Despite the fact that I continued to stink at the violin, it still was kind of fun. It wasn't that I got *lost* in the music so much as that I felt *found* while performing. My ego armored by my ham bone, I was able to withstand the constant blows to my artistic vanity.

Indeed, not even getting fired from the orchestra pit at my Uncle Morris's movie theater—for reasons of both musical ineptitude and general shiftlessness—shook my faith in my own admittedly limited talents as a showman. Dusting myself off from the ignominy of getting fired by a member my own family, I went forth into the bountiful fields of Brooklyn, and got me and my fiddle another gig.

Returning to the scene of many of my adolescent crimes, I applied for a position playing at the Thursday night socials held every week for the students, parents of students, and teachers of Manual Training High School. The job, as it were, carried no money and even less respect.

Still, the gig was an excuse to get up on a cafeteria stage and scratch out notes with whichever crappy musicians and assorted no-talent no-goodniks were willing to also climb onstage. The combo on my first night playing at Manual High consisted of two drummers, a trumpet player, and me on the violin.

It may not have been the big time. It may not even have been music. But at least I didn't have to hear my Uncle Morris complaining as I labored to entertain the masses.

Not that Morris had been overly concerned by my treachery of working for free for somebody else. By this time, you see, Uncle Morris was having his own problems with a stagestruck child. Like me, my cousin Jimmy, Morris's son, had also come under the magic spell of the Brooklyn vaudeville comics.

Unlike me, however, Jimmy was a scholarly type who analytically surveyed the entire comedy field before deciding on a favorite. In the end, Jimmy picked a comic named David D. Hall, who was known onstage as "D. D. H.?"

I never learned what the question mark was for—I guess D. D. H.? was working on some cosmic level that transcended the spiritual limits of Brooklyn. His shtick, meantime, was as broad as Sophie Tucker. Wearing a judge's black robe and a professor's tasseled mortarboard, D. D. H.? delivered nonsensical monologues that for a time were all the rage of the vaudeville houses lucky enough to book him. Basically, he was Professor Irwin Corey during the days when Corey was still in kindergarten.

My cousin Jimmy quickly became obsessed with D. D. H.? He memorized his act, copying the exact cadences of his delivery, stutter-stepping in a carbon-copy manner of the master.

In truth, Jimmy was more like a good Elvis impersonator than an actual comic. But just as a good Elvis impersonator will never go hungry for work, Jimmy was soon getting actual penny-ante gigs as a comic around Brooklyn. I was amazed. I was impressed. And since I was family, Jimmy—always a stand-up guy—decided to tutor me in the finer points of ripping off the likes of D. D. H.?

Fifty years later, I called my cousin Jimmy, who was by now retired to Miami after a successful and respectable career in the circulation department of the *New York Post*. Did he, I asked, remember any of that lifted D. D. H.? routine?

Jimmy cleared his throat, closed the door so his wife wouldn't hear, then launched into a verbatim recitation of the monologue. It began:

> Ladies and Gentlemen, standing here, as I do, before you, without even the protection of a net, I can see by the expression on the backs of your necks that you're sorry your seats are fastened to the floor.

I know, it's not exactly killer-funny. But trust me, this stuff slayed 'em in its day. So much so, in fact, that I immediately incorporated the D. D. H.? material into the routines I'd already memorized during my own truant afternoons at the lesser vaudeville houses of Brooklyn.

By the time I turned sixteen, armed with my cache of pilfered jokes and routines, I figured I was finally ready to make my professional show-biz debut. Playing school-dance socials for the approval of my peers was nice. But I wanted and needed to make a buck.

It could literally be just a buck. But I wanted to get paid to prove that I . . . to be honest I don't know what exactly I wanted to prove by getting paid to get up on-stage. But I know I wanted to prove *something,* and this was going to be the way I proved it. (Hmm, this is scary. I'm beginning to sound like a D. D. H.? routine.)

From hanging out so much in and around the vaudeville houses, I knew that the best bet for a newcomer to break in was through the good graces of a fellow named Solly Shore. Solly, it seemed, booked all the so-called "amateur" shows at all of Brooklyn's burlesque halls.

As such, Solly was a man of power, if not grace. He

wore an editor's green eye visor at all times, night and day. A compulsive knuckle-cracker, Solly always had a lit stub of a cigar clenched in his teeth. He seemed to smoke only stubs—I never saw anything more than a nubbin in his mouth.

In speech, Solly sounded just like the gravelly voiced gangster Jake Shapiro, one of the heads of Murder, Incorporated. Jake's nickname was "Gurrah," because that's how his most frequent command—"Get out of here!"—actually sounded coming out of his mouth. Anyway, you get the picture about Solly. A very strange man.

His amateur shows, meantime, were an out-and-out racket. The performers who appeared in these productions weren't amateurs, but starving and struggling show-biz people whom Solly paid three dollars apiece to take part in his phony contests. And the heavily advertised grand prize of five hundred dollars that was supposed to go to the best "amateur"? That tidy sum, of course, went right back into Solly's pocket.

The way it worked was that Solly's three-buck-a-night troupe would travel around Brooklyn theaters taking turns being lousy on amateur night. On *purpose.* Each purposefully awful act would then get the hook in the middle of its performance—and *that* would get the biggest laughs of the evening. Ah, where would show biz be without the ritual of humiliation?

Anyway, Solly would have picked out the evening's "winning" act before the show. Then, that night's winner would have been given a new stage name that would identify the act as a product of the neighborhood in which that evening's amateur contest was being held. And so, a trumpet duo from Bayonne might be renamed "The Bay

Ridge Blowers" or "the Flatbush Flugelers," depending on which neighborhood theater Solly had booked that night.

Still, performing as a member of Solly's sorry troupe was a way not only to get experience—but to actually get paid. So, one day outside a dank burlesque house near Coney Island, I boldly approached the famous impresario and introduced myself as an up-and-coming talent.

Solly, absorbed in his *Daily Racing Form,* was not interested. "Gurrah!" he growled, and I complied, running hastily down the boardwalk in the opposite direction. The next week, outside a theater in Bay Ridge, I approached Solly again. This time, in lieu of introductions, I launched immediately into my monologue.

At the end of each joke, Solly would yell out which comedian I'd stolen the gag from. I may not have been very good, but Solly at least was impressed that I stole from the masters. He also clearly saw that I wouldn't have much trouble being lousy—Solly Shore's prime employment requirement. When I finished my little rap, Solly took out his booking book.

Thumbing through several pages, he came up with a day a month down the line in which he could use my particular talents. I think it was October 10.

"Can you play the Orpheum show on October 10?" Solly said impatiently.

"Of course!" I said, not believing my ears and great fortune. True, Solly Shore was no Sol Hurok. But I wasn't exactly the Kirov Ballet either. But who cared? I was on the verge of becoming a professional.

Still, Solly seemed unimpressed by my enthusiasm.

"You're not one of them religious nuts, are you?" he asked.

"Me?" I said. "Naah."

"Good, cuz that day is Yom Kippur," Solly informed me. "We got a couple openings that day cuz a coupla our brethren who got acts ain't performing that day, no matter what I say to 'em. Friggin' fanatics."

The news that I would have to perform on Yom Kippur made even me pause. To shtick on Yom Kippur? The Jewish Day of Atonement? The day when God decides whose names shall be written in that year's editions of, respectively, the Book of Life and the Book of Death? This was heavy stuff, even for a teenage wise guy like myself.

"C'mon, kid, I got a business to run," Solly growled impatiently. "You want to be a entertainer, or are you one of them *fanatics?*"

Weighing the chance of eternal damnation against the chance to make my debut in a two-bit sham show, I made the only choice I could.

"What time should I get to the theater?" I asked. Solly gurgled, cracked his knuckles, and penciled my name into his bursting notebook.

Anyway, before I get into what happened that fateful day, we're going to have to talk about Yom Kippur for a minute.

It's the day of repentance, you know. You don't mess around on Yom Kippur. No matter how important you were, you were supposed to put down everything on Yom Kippur, sit in the synagogue, and beat your chest for your sins.

Even the no-account hard guys in our Jewish community, the ones who spent the previous 364 days chiseling customers, snarfing seafood, and chasing Gentile women, would not dare not show up at the synagogue on Yom Kippur.

So you can see how grave my decision was to break into show business on the very day when I was supposed to be praying for the future of my soul. Actually, in making my decision, I was more afraid of my father than of God.

Not that I intended for Pa to even find out that I was performing that day. Indeed, I had concocted a complicated plan that I thought would ensure that I could simultaneously make Yahweh, Yonkel Youngman, and Solly Shore happy.

My scheme was to show up at the synagogue for Yom Kippur services with my father as if nothing were unusual. After sitting for a while, I would make my move at the start of the short memorial service in which it is traditional for younger people to excuse themselves from the sanctuary and go outside and wait on the steps for the next part of the service to begin.

My plan was based on pinpoint timing. I would leave the synagogue, hang out with the gang of kids on the synagogue steps for a minute, then beat it the few blocks to the Sixteenth Street Theatre, the dingy vaudeville house where Solly Shore had booked me.

I would go onstage in my Yom Kippur finery, recite my lifted routine, then beat it back to the synagogue, Pa, and the next part of the service. There was plenty of time, I figured, to both pray for my soul and pick up a not unmeasly three bucks for telling jokes onstage.

But God, I discovered too late, *knows.* He knows which young boys are out on the synagogue steps on Yom Kippur waiting for the memorial service to end, and which are only pausing on the steps for a second en route to the nearby burlesque house.

My fatal mistake that day was telling my pal André Baruch where I was heading. Passing him on the synagogue steps, I couldn't help myself. "André, I'm off to my professional debut at the Sixteenth Street Theatre!" I said. Oops.

It must have been a death wish, me telling André, of all people. For André Baruch, age sixteen, was a guy who couldn't keep his mouth shut. André was a good guy, not a squealer or a rat. It's just that he liked to talk too much. He gave answers even when no one was asking questions. It was no mistake, believe me, that later in life André Baruch would end up as the announcer on *The Kate Smith Show*—the same program that made me a star.

I was always the opposite from André. From my earliest days, I always tended to keep my mouth shut about everybody, all the time, no matter what. This habit became a reputation—a reputation that kept me in good stead in the coming decades, as I moved my act to the classier joints on Broadway and began commingling with what used to be called, ahem, *sportsmen.*

These gangsters hung out in the same clubs I played in—you'll hear a lot more about them soon. From my very first days in show biz, this kind of wiseguy liked me hanging around his table after the joints were closed. I never flattered myself into thinking it was on account of my personality that I was allowed to sit in on some of their bull sessions. It was just that if there was one thing "sportsmen" knew about Henny Youngman, it was that he would keep his mouth shut.

Unlike, say, André Baruch. Anyway, let's go back to that fateful Yom Kippur scene. Ten minutes after my exit from shul, my father left the stuffy sanctuary in order to grab a breath of fresh air on the synagogue steps.

Passing André and the rest of my gang, Pa inquired as to his son Hen's whereabouts. "Well, well," stammered André, I was told later, "he's uhm . . ."

Then, like an arrested prisoner who's been broken under a brutal third-degree interrogation, André, witnesses later told me, spilled the bad news to my disbelieving father.

Meantime, a few blocks away, I'd just taken the stage at the Sixteenth Street Theatre. Brandishing my stolen D. D. H.? routine, I began reciting.

"Ladies and gentlemen, standing here, as I do, before you, without even the protection of a net . . ."

I noticed I was not killing the audience. Actually, from up onstage, they didn't look like an audience—they looked like an oil painting.

As I rambled, I could see Solly Shore standing in the wings, rubbing his hands together in pleasure. This kid will be very good for the troupe, I'm sure he was thinking, because this kid is very bad.

But I gamely plowed on, as only a teenage kid who doesn't have a clue about anything will do. Then, in the middle of third stanza of D. D. H.?'s monologue, the troubles came.

Some people have never been able to forget the last line spoken in *Our American Cousin* before John Wilkes Booth entered Abraham Lincoln's theater box and shot the president. Me, I can never forget the two sentences I spoke right before I was greeted with the meaning of Old Testament wrath, courtesy of Pa. Those lines were:

> Folks, I've been known to talk for hours without saying a word. I have been promised life insurance and life imprisonment. Of course, I could tell you more about myself, but there may be police in the house.

With that, I heard a loud commotion coming from the wings. "Gurrah! Gurrah!" I heard a beet-faced Solly Shore scream as the rapidly approaching figure of one of Brooklyn's finest rushed past the impresario and onto the stage. "Whataya, whataya?" Solly yelled at the charging beat cop, "dis iz a clean show, a family show!"

Running just a foot behind the policeman was Yonkel Youngman. My own father had called the heat down on me! "Whatsamatter with you?" said the cop as he grabbed my ear and dragged me offstage.

I recognized him as Patrolman Feeney from the neighborhood. Despite his heritage, Feeney was well acquainted with the import of Yom Kippur. And like the rest of our mixed neighborhood, Feeney was able to express himself in a variety of tongues.

"Fer Chrissakes, kid," Feeney intoned, "doncha know it's *yontif?*"

Once outside, my father took over the ear-pulling duties. He didn't say a word as he pulled me back to the synagogue. There was enough left in the Yom Kippur service, he felt, that I still had time to reclaim my soul.

To be honest, I'm not sure what hurt him more—

that I had desecrated the holy holiday, or that I'd obviously rejected all his tutorings about high culture. He'd offered me the subtle tastes of the opera and ballet, and I'd thrown in my lot with burlesque kings who wear green eyeshades even when it's dark.

Even through the horror and shame, I learned a valuable lesson that day, a lesson that to my mind is the First Commandment of Show Business. No, Solly Shore spluttered to me when I came back to see him the next day, I would not be receiving my promised three dollars.

"No play," Solly gurgled, "no pay." Curiously, the burlesque audience had loved the part in my act where the cop ran in and dragged me offstage. Nowadays, on those rare occasions when I affect a pose as a Greenwich Village artiste, I bring up my debut as one of the earliest-known examples of performance art.

Comédie véritée I call it—ooh, the college boys all love it, and take notes, and then go on to write their textbooks on how comedy works. Meantime, the way comedy *really* works is just as Solly Shore told me that long ago Yom Kippur Day.

"No play," Solly said one more time, cracking his knuckles, "no pay."

Remember that, kids who want to go into show business. It could save your life someday.

CHAPTER SIX

In Which Our Young Hero Takes Leave of School, Meets the Telephone Booth Indians, and Learns How to Make a Pair of Pants Last (Make the Coat and Vest First)

Unfortunately, the enduring wisdom of Solly Shore's no-play-no-pay dictum was the only lesson I bothered to memorize in those long-ago school days. Indeed, my formal education at Brooklyn's Manual Training High School came to an abrupt and premature end only a couple of months after my sensational Yom Kippur Day performance.

My death sentence from secondary education arrived, I remember, in a pale blue envelope delivered by our mailman to my pa. The gist of the letter was that neither Manual High's classrooms nor detention halls could apparently reform my wise-guy ways. Hence, the letter concluded, my continued presence was no longer deemed necessary at the school.

(This whole incident of Pa getting this letter reminds me of that scene in Martin Scorsese's movie *GoodFellas*. You know, the part where the letter to the little wise guy's parents from his school is intercepted because the truant kid is already connected?)

My God, I wonder what would have happened to me if *I* had been connected, if that letter hadn't reached my father. Maybe I could have been another Meyer Lansky. More likely, I would have ended up vacuuming some tough guy's pool in Miami Beach. In any case, rent *GoodFellas*. That Scorsese is the real thing, no phony baloney from that guy. And besides, I'm in the movie, playing a cameo as myself. You know, I think I did okay. Me. In an art picture, fer Chrissakes!

Anyway, where was I before I took that commercial interruption? Oh yes, getting kicked out of school. Anyway, I wasn't too upset. I mean, with my absence and detention record, I was out of school already, de facto.

Please note that the gratuitous use of the words "de facto" was thrown in in the memory of Noodles Bazis of the old candy-store gang, who used to throw "de facto" into every conversation, no matter the context. "Babe Herman is the Dodgers' captain, de facto," Noodles might say, or, "She's my girlfriend, de facto." Rest in peace, Noodles.

Hmm, digressions, digressions, I hope you, my dear reader, don't mind. When you get to be my age, you're allowed to wander a bit, huh? So many names, so many faces, so many memories, so much time. . . .

Anyway, as I was saying, I had just gotten the boot

from school. Still, I took the news that I'd been kicked out of Manual High with amazing grace. Pa, meantime, reacted with predictable pain and fury. To him, my expulsion from school was the meanest insult I could have thrown at the Youngman family crest.

(Of course, there is no Youngman family crest. If there was, our shield would probably consist of a shmear of shtetl dirt, a swatch of sweatshop cloth, and a page from the libretto to *Carmen.*)

Before my expulsion, Pa was usually all-forgiving. In time, he even forgave me for performing in a schlock vaudeville house on Yom Kippur. In that case, he forgave by persuading himself that I had gone to work for Solly Shore as a political act against organized religion. "I'm a freethinker myself," he told me when he announced that I was finally out of the High Holiday doghouse.

But getting booted from Manual High was different. It was *school.* It was *books.* It was *culture.* Oh, he told me, what he would give to change places with me, to be able to spend all day reading and writing and discussing. And what, he wanted to know, did I do with this gift of time and youth? I throw it away like yesterday's newspaper.

I shrugged. Pa continued.

No, he told me, he didn't mind knowing that his son would never grow up to be a captain of industry or finance. Being poor and honest was one thing he fully understood and respected. But to be unread? To be uninterested in scholarly argument?

It was also obvious, Pa continued, that I wasn't going to become a doctor. Or a lawyer. Or (sigh) a concert violinist. I wasn't a balancer of other people's ledgers, and I didn't exactly have the temperament for eight-to-six office work. "It's time," he said, "to think practical."

After issuing that announcement in our tiny kitchen a fortnight after I was kicked out of school, Pa motioned for me to follow him into his office. Pa actually had two rooms in the apartment that he called his "office." The first was his and Ma's bedroom, which became an "office" whenever Pa went in alone and closed the door to think.

For example, say Ma yelled for Pa to come out from the bedroom and say hello to his mother-in-law. Pa would yell from behind the door, "Can't you see I'm working in the office?"

Pa's other office was in that great and historic Jewish research library . . . the bathroom. He'd spend hours in there, reading texts on Fauvism and Hegel and Dr. Mendel's peas. Meantime, I would have to pee. "Pa, open up!" I'd yell, banging on the door. "Yes, yes," I'd hear him say distractedly through the frame, lost in a daydreamer's fog.

But Pa was no airhead as he herded me into the bedroom office on that long-ago day of reckoning. Suddenly, he was a believer in, of all things, the practical. Let me tell you, it is an interesting sight to see a lifelong *luftmensh* suddenly launch into a very good imitation of a man giving a heartfelt sermon about pragmatism. I got to admit, Pa was pretty moving.

He began with a line I thought was so funny that I've used it in various forms as a gag in my act for sixty-plus years. "Hen," my father started, "you're sixteen years old. Soon, you'll be seventeen. (Pause.) If I let you." I swear, I thought I heard a snare drum's rim shot as Yonkel delivered his unintentional punch line.

The point, my father lectured, was that it was time to figure out what I was going to do with the rest of my life. What had saved the Youngmans over the generations, Pa's lecture continued, was a *trade.* "When I had to run from Russia," he explained, "I knew I could make a living wherever I went in the world. I would be welcome wherever people needed hats and caps."

"But, Pa," I interrupted, "when you moved to Paris, you worked in the opera claque."

"That was different, I was young," Pa shot back. "And don't interrupt. Knowing how to make a cap, not knowing how to clap, is what gave me my freedom. When I wanted to leave Paris for London, I just got up and went. And *there,* I made caps.

"And if you think I was brave to come to America," he continued, "I wasn't. Because I had a trade. And I made enough out of it to bring the rest of the family to America. That's what a trade can mean to a man."

"But, Pa," I pointed out, "Uncle *Morris* brought the family over."

"Oh, excuse me, Mr. District Attorney," Pa said. "May I continue?"

"Pa," I said, "I don't *want* to go into the cap-and-hat business."

"I wouldn't let you," Pa said. "It's not good enough for my Hen."

No, he had a different vocation in mind for me that would combine both idealism and practicality. Even if his son Hen couldn't write books, and wasn't particularly interested in reading books, perhaps I could just *print* the books. I was, he said, going to a printer.

"It's an honorable trade," Pa said. "A man has to make a living."

He even had a battle plan. It seemed I could immediately enroll in the Brooklyn Vocational Trade School, a melting pot of working-class Irish, Italian, Polish, black, and Jewish grease-monkeys-in-training.

I agreed to go, mostly because I was so impressed by the fact that my father had obviously spent so much more time thinking about my future than I had. The alternative, I knew, was to risk becoming that word that all Jewish boys of my generation grew up fearing.

If you don't read your lessons and honor your parents, we were all told, then you know what you'll end up as? A *bum.*

Bum. I don't know if the power of this word translates over the decades, but it used to mean a combination of shnorrer and gonif and every other bad word you can think of in Yiddish.

Yes, it was a fearsome word. As an example of its power, let me point to my neighborhood friend Markle. Markle's father, originally from a shtetl two villages down from Pa's, sold used cardboard boxes on Plymouth Avenue; his family was as poor as mine.

Markle, however, was a student. He graduated high school at fifteen, went to CCNY for free, and got a full ride through NYU Medical School courtesy of the army. After medical school, the army sent Markle down to a post in Galveston. When his army time was up, Markle wired his Old World parents in Brooklyn that he had been offered a prestigious medical post in Dallas.

"Come home, bum," rocketed back the response from the old man. And Markle came.

"You're no bum," my own father said to me when I told him yes, I would become a printer. "You're my son."

It was a nice moment. I hope in these descriptions that I haven't painted a picture of my father as some kind of buffoon. Because he really did care. Not only about his family, but about what he used to melodramatically call "the family of man." He took very seriously all those lessons about social utopia that he'd studied in the bathroom.

It was one thing, he often told me, to drink schnapps with his socialist immigrant buddies and argue about Emma Goldman's poetry. But it was quite another, he said, to take those principles to heart and try to make a little difference in the world.

Hence, Pop's humanistic solution to a problem I brought home a couple of weeks after starting Brooklyn Vocational Trade School. I've already described the school's population of assorted lugnuts, blockheads, and chronic underachievers. What I learned upon arrival at the school, however, was that our class also consisted of a large percentage of orphans.

These kids with no families had been sent here for training by all of the Brooklyn orphanages. After these unfortunate kids received their vocational certificates, they were finally dispatched from their sad institutions into the real world.

You could always tell the orphans at school—every day at noon, they were the ones sitting at the lunch table without any lunches. I felt bad for them, and wanted to give what I could. But there were so many orphans sitting there, silent, and sullen, that there wasn't nearly enough of my lunch to pass around.

I brought this impossible problem of long division

to my father. Pa rubbed his chin like Solomon, snapped his fingers, and announced a solution. He knew that students at Brooklyn Vocational Trade School were allowed to go home for lunch. Tomorrow, my father instructed me, round up the orphans at noon and bring them over here.

Pa was prepared when I arrived home the next afternoon with my ragged band of ten Irish, black, Chinese, and Italian orphans. He'd purchased, I saw, six cans of sardines, three loaves of bread, and five New York newspapers filled with enough sports pages and comics sections for all.

I don't know if I ever saw my father so happy as when he invited those boys into our kitchen for a nice sardine sandwich and some equally filling talk. He enjoyed himself so much that every couple weeks he would order me to bring the gang of orphans back for lunch. The old man was definitely all right.

All he ever wanted was for me to grow up and be *comfortable.* Ah, "comfortable," a word loaded with as much meaning to my generation of Jews as "bum," "doctor," or "prince." And what exactly did it mean to be "comfortable?" No one, it seemed, was ever quite clear on a specific definition.

Even with his apartment and movie-house and liquor-store ownerships, for instance, my uncle Morris didn't think of himself as rich. He was *comfortable.* By the same token, my father, with his poverty-line income and rented cold-water flat, didn't think of himself as poor. He was *comfortable.*

Did you hear about the old Jewish guy who was hit by a taxi outside the Fontainebleau Hotel in Miami

Beach? A crowd gathers at the scene as an ambulance wails in the distance. Someone brings the old guy a pillow and blanket, and he is propped and covered. An older woman leans over the old guy and asks, "Are you comfortable?"

"I make a living."

And so, my father figured, the route to comfortability for his errant son would be the printing press.

Show business, however, was still vaguely on my mind. Not because I was searching for glory and stardom, but because I figured that I might still be able to make a spare buck in the biz.

Gee, that sounds quaint now—the biz. These days, every hoo-ha in show business now refers to his trade as "the *industry.*" Hoo-ha.

And where did I pick up this idea that I might be able to make small change performing? On Broadway, of course, only a subway ride away in Manhattan.

It was there, in the dingy offices of the scores of music publishing houses that operated in the theater district, that I heard the good word. With a hardworking agent, I learned, a musical combo could make five dollars a head a night playing around town. That beat Solly Shore's three-dollar rigged amateur hours by a good margin.

I learned this secret while on duty as the fiddle player in my Uncle Morris's sorry little movie-theater orchestra. Early on, the older woman who plinked the decomposing piano in our two-man band had tipped me off that in Manhattan we could get free sheet music of the day's current hits.

All I had to do was take the subway to Publishers Row on Broadway, go into those disheveled offices, and tell them I led the orchestra in a large Brooklyn movie theater. With those words, I learned, I could get gratis copies of the hottest arrangements.

These were the songs that the publishers were pushing the hardest. These companies made a lot of money on their sheet music in those days, and they'd promote their product by hocking vaudeville stars or theater orchestras to play their songs.

So, sitting there daydreaming one day in my printing class, I figured an easy solution to finding some more dough. I'd get up a combo. We'd get free sheet music of the newest hits. We'd get gigs. We'd play the free sheet music of the newest hits. We'd get paid.

And so, after classes at the vocational school, I started putting together a little band. Though talent was definitely not a prerequisite to be considered for my quartet, I didn't discriminate against an applicant so blessed.

In the end, I even found a neighborhood fellow with actual musical ability. His name was Mike Riley, and he played the craziest trombone I'd ever heard. I first spied Riley when his church marching band passed me during a Columbus Day parade. At the time, Riley was intoning some interesting riffs that I suspected were not in the sheet music he'd been provided by St. Michael's Catholic Church.

I followed as the band veered from the street and into their church at Fifth Avenue and Fifty-ninth Street in Brooklyn. I talked Riley into my combo as he took off his ridiculous-looking marching-band hat. I'm glad I did. For though Riley is pretty much forgotten now, no one who heard his magic trombone could believe how that sonofabitch played.

Ten years later, Riley was a major star on "The Street." That, of course, was Fifty-second Street—the Manhattan block between Fifth and Sixth avenues where the finest nightclubs in the city served up the country's best jazz musicians, comics, torch singers, and female impersonators.

It was while playing the Onyx Club on The Street that Riley wrote the song that I thought would make him go down in history—"The Music Goes Round and Round." For decades, every band in the country played that song on New Year's Eve. But now? I don't know. Does anybody remember the great Mike Riley?

The other members of the quartet were not as memorable. To be honest, I can't even remember them. Besides Riley and me, the group was an ever-changing assortment of neighborhood guys whose primary qualification was that they owned their own instruments.

The name of our quartet was "the Swanee Syncopators." I know it sounds ridiculous now, but at the time we all thought it sang. We came up with that name for a variety of reasons. Today, the first reason we took the moniker probably seems at least offensive and probably racist.

But at the time the combo was formed, one of the most asked-for forms of popular music were so-called "coon songs." Yes, that's what everybody called them, and just about every combo had a couple of that kind of tune in its repertoire. Anyway, the one thing all these songs seemed to have in common was a lyric extolling the Swanee River. Hence, the birth of the Swanee Syncopators. I'm not proud of it, but that's what happened.

There was another reason, however, to identify ourselves with the Swanee. My cousin Jimmy and some friends had recently bought into a dinky upstate New York resort called the Swan Lake Inn. With a band name like ours, I was sure Jimmy would eventually hire us for a gig or two among the vacationing New York City Jews who were rapidly turning rural Sullivan County into something you might have heard of called the borscht belt.

In other venues, however, the combo would have other names. Always looking for a home-field advantage with our sometimes-unruly audiences, the group might turn on successive weekends from the Swanee Syncopators to the Bay Ridge Society Orchestra to the Flatbush Five.

Granted, that last name was a little strange considering we were only a quartet. Still, I thought it sounded poetic, and none of the locals we played for in that neighborhood bordering Ebbets Field ever seemed to mind.

Finding a name was easier then finding a free place to practice. For a time, we tried using the roof of the tailor shop that was next door to my family's apartment. Within minutes of unpacking, however, ungrateful neighbors from my own building would usually begin raining a barrage of rotten fruit down upon us.

A solution to our rehearsal-space dilemma was soon offered by our pianist, a kid named Stuey "Chopsticks" Bloom. He got the nickname "Chopsticks" because, no kidding, Bloom could actually play that famous kid song on the piano while wearing boxing gloves. For bar bets only, however. For Chrissakes, our combo was no novelty act!

Anyway, Bloom said the combo could use his family's

parlor to practice in. When the group convened at Bloom's address on Brooklyn's Fifth Avenue, we discovered that his "parlor" was in fact his father's mortuary.

Bloom's father, a music enthusiast, eagerly ushered us into his funeral parlor and instructed us to go ahead and practice our dance tunes as loudly as we wanted. As the group unpacked, Mr. Bloom went about the business of checking in one of his newly shrouded customers. We tried to practice, we did, but our arrangements just seemed to lack a little zip every time we played in the death room.

In time, we learned that the best place to practice was on the subway to and from a gig. We'd set up in the last car of the train, and play for the conductor. Once in a while a rider would toss a nickel into our instrument cases. Now ain't that living? To be paid for rehearsing?

Oftentimes, however, these subway jams were the only rehearsals the band would get all week. All the guys were enrolled in some sort of school, and all of us also had afternoon jobs. Any extra time we had to practice tootling together was considered pure gravy.

My form of extracurricular employment was working inside a printing booth in the basement of the Kresge's Department Store in downtown Brooklyn. This was the exact establishment where Pa had a job painting signs. Nepotism, however, didn't get me in.

I'd been hired by a local printer who had leased the basement box from Kresge's, then installed me as the booth's flunky proprietor. My stand specialized in the printing of cut-rate business cards and letterheads for shady businesses specializing in fly-by-night services. Grifters, crooked ex-cops starting private-detective agencies, lawyers with highly questionable credentials—ah, these were my people.

My clientele was largely made up of what used to be called "Telephone Booth Indians." These guys got the nickname because their actual business offices consisted of nothing more than a phone booth outside Kresge's. Of course, the marks whom the Telephone Booth Indians were calling didn't know this.

Here's how it worked. A Telephone Booth Indian calls a mark and/or business contact from his booth. If the mark wasn't there, the Indian would leave a message and a request to be called back at the phone booth's number.

After hanging up, the Indian would stay in the phone booth so no one else could tie up the line. With the cradle pushed down to keep the line open, he would keep the receiver to his head, and mime a conversation. Civilians angling for a pay phone wouldn't bother the seemingly busy man in the booth.

And the line wouldn't be busy when the Indian's client called back. "Hello, Shmendrick Investments," the Indian could now answer the phone, the mark none the wiser that he'd reached a phone booth, not an office. *Capisce?*

Down in the Kresge's basement, I became a student in the college of characters. With these wiseguys, I learned, the nicer the shoes, the worse the character. Alcoholics, I discovered, frequently missed a day of shaving. Track rats and dice hounds could always be identified by their ridiculous hats and shiny pants. Skirt-chasers always smelled of their own cologne, even when they didn't have any on. Con men tended to have expensive watchbands and cheap watches. 'Twas a sentimental education, no?

I had been granted a ringside seat at a carnival of human weakness in all its mismatched splendor. True, my actual job description was just to print business cards that said things like "established 1879" for our clients' just-formed companies. But my real job was just to watch.

Understanding the thought patterns of this kind of character proved especially useful when I moonlighted for a while from Kresge's as a summons server. I'd get fifty cents for each summons I actually managed to get into a servee's hands, which frequently was no small feat.

The toughest cookie I ever had to serve was a gonif named Callaghan. I literally spent weeks chasing the sonofabitch all over Brooklyn in a vain attempt to get him to just touch that summons. To hell with the fifty cents —I wasn't going to let this portly middle-aged Irishman outsmart this street-smart teenage Jew.

I finally nailed him when I noticed that the bowling alley he owned had a phone near the front window. I called him up from a phone booth across the street and said, "Excuse me, Mr. Callaghan? I've got some money for you. Can you hold on a minute?" Callaghan held on long enough for me to hustle across the street and place the summons in his vest pocket. Justice is served!

So I chased, and when I was working in the Kresge's basement, I watched. Luckily, a dearth of actual paying customers who need printing done gave me plenty of time to pay attention. Or work on my own schemes. My first, and best, was a product I called "fun cards."

When business was slow, I took to printing up jokes on the back of blank business cards. I'd bundle the joke cards into sets of ten, and sell them at the store, or at school, or wherever I happened to be that day. I was a good enough schmoozer that on my best days I could sell as many as forty packs.

I even came to my printed-up jokes in a kosher manner. Or so I thought. Every week, you see, *Variety* would print in its vaudeville section a feature called "Released Jokes." I, in my infinite teenage wisdom, took this to mean that a vaudevillean was done with these jokes and had "released" them to the public. Hence, I figured, it was okay for me to print up these gags on my fun cards.

A few decades later, however, I finally learned the meaning of *Variety*'s old "Released Jokes" feature. These jokes, it turned out, were the ones the editors of the showbiz bible felt were so stale, ancient, and awful that they should forever be struck from telling.

I'd known at the time that some of the jokes I was printing up were slightly moldy. Still, the customers seemed to like them, especially the joke that I always printed on card one.

"Do you want to know how to make a pair of pants last?" read that gag. "Make the coat and vest first." Ouch. Double ouch.

I was young. What the hell did I know? Enough to know that if somebody wanted to pay for these mildewed jokes, then I'd provide. *"Nem di Gelt,"* remember, *get the money.*

CHAPTER SEVEN

A Historic Moment in Twentieth-Century Comedy: I Meet My Future Mother-in-Law

I had other diversions besides selling "fun cards" during my downtime in Kresge's basement. One way I killed time was to work the phone in my tiny printer's box in an attempt to line up gigs for the Swanee Syncopators.

The group always split the money from our engagements evenly. But whoever actually *got* the job was allowed to lead the combo for the evening. I liked being out front whenever possible, waving my violin bow to the musicians behind me like Guy Lombardo or Paul Whiteman. So, driven by visions of showboating, I played the phone like an instrument. Dialing again and again, I searched for a gig, any gig, that paid.

However, my favorite pastime down in Kresge's basement was to secretly stare at the exceedingly pretty Irish girl working the phonograph and sheet-music booth directly across the aisle from me. This girl was seventeen, with red hair, freckles, and the kind of laugh that you knew came from Eire, not the Diaspora.

As such, she was the kind of seventeen-year-old girl whom my mother would politely say hello to on first meeting, then excuse herself to the kitchen and turn on the gas pipe. To summon the courage to ask this non-Jewish girl out on a date would, I'd been led to believe, bring immediate and permanent shame down upon my parents.

My folks would have to change their names and move out of Brooklyn. When asked about whatever happened to their eldest son, Hen, Mà would have to stammer, "We used to have a son named Hen. But no more."

Or so I imagined. Actually, I don't think the problem would have come from my father. He was a freethinker, after all, a man who prided himself on his advanced social views. Indeed, later in life he took a keen interest in the career of Veronica Lake, who, if you remember, didn't exactly look like Barbra Streisand. Anyway, I know Pa would have eventually welcomed any woman I loved, be she Jewish or not, into our home.

With Ma, I'm not so sure. Now there are many stories concerning the supposedly all-forgiving ways of Jewish mothers when it comes to their wayward sons. My favorite such tale is even true, which is amazing when you consider the number of bullshit stories that have circulated over the years about the Jews in their American ghettos.

Anyway, this story of a Jewish boy and his mother involves the notorious Sam "Killer" Kaplan, the number-one triggerman for Murder, Inc., the Jewish gang that ran out of Brooklyn's Brownsville section. I think it was around 1933 when Kaplan got into the wrong end of a shoot-out across the street from Cohen's Appliances.

Critically shot, Killer still managed to crawl the three blocks to his mother's house. Bleeding all over the landing, he hoisted himself up the stairs, pounded on the door, and screamed, "Mama, it's me, Sammy! I'm hurt bad!"

"Sit down and eat," his mother said, opening the door. "Later we'll talk."

With one notable exception, my ma was the exact same way with me. I could have come home, told her I'd just kidnapped Henry Ford, stowed him in the coal bin, and was ready to shoot the mogul unless my ransom demands were met. "I understand how you feel," Ma would have said. "That Henry Ford is an anti-Semite. Would a little *kugel* make you feel better?"

But Ma might not have forgiven the sin of interdating, let alone intermarriage. Though the Youngmans didn't discuss this touchy issue much—nobody did—let us just say that in my family, there was intense pressure not to became attached to a Gentile woman. And so, I had to content myself by silently mooning from across the Kresge's aisle at this Irish beauty with the mile-long smile.

Me, of glib temperament and a head full of pretty lousy jokes, could never untangle my tongue whenever I saw this girl. I was beyond stammering. Saying "hello" seemed impossible. "Good morning" was out of the question. She had struck me silent.

Anyway, I consoled myself, nothing could ever happen, even if I could somehow work up the courage to start up a conversation with the beautiful sheet-music woman. After all, I imagined, the pressure she had not to go out with Jews or Italians was as much as mine not to go out with the Irish. And let's face it. From her perspective, I wasn't exactly O Danny Boy.

Or so I thought.

Finally, circumstances arose that made it necessary for me to speak to the red-haired Irish queen laboring across the Kresge's aisle from me. It was a true emergency—there was a potential gig hanging on the line.

The man on the phone with me at that moment was a booker for a Coney Island dance hall. I had already been working the line in the printing booth for an hour that after-school afternoon in a vain attempt to line up a job for the Swanee Syncopators for the coming weekend.

This booker was one of those guys who called everybody "genius." "Good morning, genius," he'd greet you, or "*Nu,* genius?" It's funny—about once a decade I run into somebody who calls one and all "genius." I hate it. Call me Henny. Call me Mr. Youngman. You can even call me *putz*. But don't call me "genius."

But I digress. Anyway, I'm talking to this "genius" booker. He tells me he'd just had a band cancel a gig that was slated for the next Saturday night on Coney Island. The job, he said, would pay thirty dollars—five bucks a head, I figured, tallying up how many men I could scrounge up that night for our always-expanding-and-contracting band.

There was just one problem. The booker had never heard us play, and wanted an earful before he'd hire us. "What do you mean, 'hear us'?" I asked, assuming my best prima donna voice. "*We* don't audition."

"No, you don't have to audition," he said. "It's just that I was told this number was where your band rehearsed. Let me hear a little."

I'm sure he *was* told that this number was where the Swanee Syncopators rehearsed. As per the philosophy of the Telephone Booth Indians working the phones around the corner, it doesn't look good for a professional entertainer to have his business number located in the basement of a Kresge's. You wanted bookers to think you were so good—and highly paid—that you didn't *need* a day job.

Okay, so what can I do? I've got a thirty-dollar gig on the line waiting to hear a sample of the snappy tunes he'll be hearing this Saturday night, and I'm . . . in the basement of Kresge's.

Necessity being the mother of most things a little shady, I called out to my beloved Irish lass working across the aisle at the sheet-music and phonograph-records booth. She was shocked by my "Excuse me, miss"—smitten mute; I still hadn't managed to utter one word to her in all the months we had worked so near each other.

Cupping my hand over the telephone, I asked the Irish woman if she would be so kind as to play a dance record on her demonstration phonograph. She nodded, befuddled, and put on a number played by none other than Rudy Vallee and his Connecticut Yankees.

"Okay," I told the booker, "I'm in the rehearsal space

now. Here we are." I held the phone in the direction of the record player, which continued to emit the talents of Mr. Vallee.

"Okay," the booker grumbled, "you'll do, genius. By the way, what's the name of your group?"

Remembering where we'd be playing, I told him "the Coney Island Ramblers."

"Nice coincidence, genius," said the booker, hanging up the phone.

I put my phone back in the cradle, and looked across the aisle at the redhead who'd gotten me a gig without even knowing my name. Eyeing me suspiciously, she slowly took Rudy Vallee off the phonograph. To hell with tradition, I said to myself. I was going to ask this Irish girl out.

"Excuse me, miss," I stammered, "would you like to hear my band play this Saturday night in Coney Island?"

"It depends," she said. "You're not Jewish, are you?"

I knew it. Even if she said yes, I'd still have a gang of her brothers named Seamus and Paddy chasing after me with brickbats.

"Yes," I said, the romance apparently dead before it had even begun.

"Good," she said, introducing herself as Sadie Cohen.

"Co-han?" I inquired, "like the great Irishman and songsmith George M.?"

"No," said the red-haired beauty, "Co-hen, like that great Jew and men's trousers salesman my pa." Orthodox, no less, it turned out. My parents, it seemed, wouldn't have to disown me.

For the next several minutes, I coaxed, wheedled, and pleaded with Sadie to join me for that Saturday night's gig on Coney Island. As I babbled, all those months of nervous muteness coming to an end, Sadie just eyed me and shook her head.

She was incredibly soft-spoken and innocent. She was also very reluctant to give me, a big-mouthed wise guy, a simple date. The only boys Sadie had ever been out with were a couple of her equally innocent schoolmates—all of whom planned on respectable careers in the needle trades or, if they were lucky, as accountants.

But to go out with a musician? A high school dropout who spent his time in the basement of Kresge's *shpritzing* with the characters?

"Okay," she finally said. "But wear a tie when you pick me up. For Mama."

Papa, it turned out, had died when Sadie was eleven. But not before he'd provided the Cohen family's Flatbush flat with the block's only chandelier, as well as an upright piano and an Edison phonograph. The Cohens weren't the Rothschilds—hell, they probably hadn't even made it to the middle class yet—but to my eyes, I'd arrived. My God, they even had hot water!

Answering the door, Sadie's ma looked me over as if I were a piece of suspect merchandise. True, the tie I'd scrounged up as per Sadie's command wasn't exactly flattering. Indeed, it looked like one of those soupstained objects of humiliation that fancy restaurants make gentlemen who forgot their ties wear so everyone in the dining room knows what a *shmeckel* they are.

I tried to small-talk Mrs. Cohen with a rap that probably sounded like the 1924 equivalent of Eddie Haskell, that phony apple-polisher on *Leave It to Beaver.* Somehow, Sadie's ma didn't buy my soft soap. For years, I'd seen that very look in her eyes in my very own home. "Bum," I knew she was thinking, "BUM!" It would take years before that look went away from Mrs. Cohen's eyes.

I didn't really care though, for I'd managed to land a date with the most beautiful girl I'd ever worked up the courage to say boo to. Opening the door and sweeping Sadie out of the tenement in a manner that I thought resembled that of a southern aristocrat, we were welcomed by the band, loitering out on the pavement. "Your carriage awaits," I told Sadie, sweeping my arms down Chauncey Street in the direction of the Coney Island–bound subway.

That night turned out to be a memorable gig. With Sadie watching, I led the band through its paces like a man possessed. I knew we stank, everybody in the band knew we stank, usually our audiences knew we stank. But for some reason—I like to think it was Sadie—we cooked that night.

So much so that after our performance a reporter for *Variety* came up to me, asked about the particulars of the band, and jotted down a couple of notes. Now that the gig was over, I discarded our "Coney Island Ramblers" moniker, and told the reporter proudly that we were the Swanee Syncopators.

After the show, we all boarded the last car on the subway for the ride back from the shore to our assorted tenements. The band was so exhilarated by our performance that night that we all took out our instruments and started playing over the rumble of the subway wheels. With Sadie watching and smiling, we ran through some of our favorite numbers—things like Billy Rose's hit "Barney Google" and "Yes, We Have No Bananas."

As our car trundled through Brooklyn, it filled up with assorted citizens, Saturday night drunks, and curious subway motormen. Many sang along, some even threw a nickel or dime into an empty instrument case. Whenever a band member got up to get off at his stop, the rest of the Syncopators held him back. This wonderful night wasn't going to end just yet.

Looking at Sadie, and then at my tootling band, and then at our sing-along audience, I thought to myself, I'm *happy.*

We played the entire way to Times Square, where the band finally detrained to wander and wonder at the sights of Broadway. Yeah, we all said, slapping each other's backs, someday this band was going to *own* this part of town.

Idiots, all of us.

Finally, the band dispersed. I took Sadie's hand, and we walked toward Central Park. She'd never been to Manhattan before, she told me. That thought seemed so touching and innocent that I was overcome. I did what I shouldn't have done. I kissed her on the cheek. To this day, I can still remember what she said.

"How," Sadie asked, "can you do this in front of all of these people?"

It was a question bookers and critics would ask me for decades. But now, all I wanted to do was . . . check my watch. Jesus, I was two hours late in bringing Sadie back home. Her mother probably had a posse with torches out looking for her by now.

"Bum," her mother's eyes said to me when I finally ushered Sadie back up the steps to her Flatbush apartment. BUMBUMBUM.

"Mama," Sadie said, "a man from *Variety* interviewed Hen tonight."

Mrs. Cohen, apparently not in thrall to higher literature, was unimpressed. Staring right at me, Mrs. Cohen said, "Thank you very much, Mr. Youngman, that will be all."

I then heard her mutter under her breath an old Yiddish saying. *"Beser a falsher 'gut morgn,' "* she mumbled, *"eyder an emeser 'shvarts yor.' "* Which means, "Better an insincere 'good morning' than a real 'go to hell.' "

Who could blame her? Even with the lowered standards of the day, I knew I wasn't exactly a catch. Still, I labored in my quest to woo my Sadie. Most days I brought her candy and flowers in the basement of Kresge's. I mooned from my booth, and she blushed in hers.

I even resorted to propaganda. When the teeny article came out in *Variety* about the band's performance on Coney Island, I splurged and bought two copies—one for my folks, and one for Mrs. Cohen.

Buried back in *Variety* with the vaudeville obits was our blurb, dated July 1924, set in just a little-bit-bigger print than agate type. It was my first review, and one of the only ones I've ever kept.

HEN YOUNGMAN AND SYNCOPATORS PLAY CONEY ISLAND BOARDWALK reads the long-faded headline. "The seven piece combination"—I guess back then you didn't have to be able to count to be a reporter—"is making a specialty of novelty stuff, including eccentric clowning, singing and dancing. Hen Youngman, violinist and leader, is also doing comedy songs."

The review was nice, but I was actually horrified to see my name in print. "Hen" was what everybody in the world had called me since I was a little kid, but I had never actually seen the nickname typed out before. It looked terrible, I thought, especially for show business. Hens lay eggs, don't you know. It may have *sounded* okay, but laid down in print, "Hen" looked like the handle of a first-class *putz*.

Then and there I decided to change it. I wasn't going to revert to my given name—"Henry Youngman," I thought, sounded like a dentist, not a bandleader. And so, I decided to merge Henry with Hen.

Ladies and gentlemen, let me present Henny Youngman.

Besides convincing me to alter my first name, the review in *Variety* also got us a few more gigs. Not so many that I was able to quit Kresge's basement, but I was getting enough extra work to keep Sadie in flowers and candy.

Oh, she was such a beautiful, nice, and simple girl. After her pa died when she was eleven, Sadie just put her nose down in a book and didn't lift it up until she graduated from high school with honors.

But in those days not even straight-"A" daughters of Jewish immigrants thought about going to college. After graduating high school, she got a job at Kresge's keeping the store's books—she was the only Jew allowed to work in the joint's office. From there she transferred to sheet music and phonographs . . . and me.

To the day she died, may she rest in peace, Sadie never really understood the fancy-pants world of show business, with all its broad smiles and stabs in the back and assorted other intrigues that make it such a ridiculous way to make a living. From the beginning, however, she tried to understand. She accompanied me on many of the band's gigs, sometimes reluctantly.

Remembering the smash the Swanee Syncopators made the first time I brought Sadie, I came to believe she was our lucky charm. She was, as I said in a joke I told for decades, my million-dollar baby. Before taxes.

One early gig, however, I most certainly did not invite Sadie to attend. After that big Coney Island show, I was approached by a fellow representing the Old Fall River Line of boats. The company, it seemed, ran night boats from New York to Boston, and was always in need of on-deck entertainment.

Few of the line's customers ever got off in Boston, however, for the Old Fall River Line was actually a floating hot-sheet motel. *Shtupping,* not shipping, was the reason the line was in existence.

A cabin or board on the night boat, you see, was cheaper than a hotel, and couples looking for a tumble got the added benefit of the nice sea-salt air. Not to mention the chance to hear sparkling entertainers plying their trade on the poop deck.

Unfortunately, Old Fall River Line customers seemed no more interested in hearing music than in disembarking when we landed in Boston. Once in a while, usually on the return trip to New York, some guy would emerge from below deck to smoke a cigarette or get a second wind, listen to a few bars of our lonely music, then go back below for round two, or three, or four. Animals, I tell you.

No, I just don't think Sadie would have approved of that engagement.

She had no qualms, however, when the band was

invited to spend the next summer playing the Catskills. As I'd hoped, my comic-struck cousin Jimmy Kaplan, Uncle Morris's son, got us hooked up with a bunch of Brooklyn grade-school teachers who'd bought a little resort up in the mountains called the Swan Lake Inn. To this day, I think we got the job because of the Swanee Syncopator's convenient name, and not because we had any discernable musical or social ability.

"Who needs musical ability working the Catskills?" my cousin Jimmy said to me. "What they need is *tumult!*"

"Henny," one of the Swan Lake Inn proprietors said as he shook my hand to ice the band's engagement, "welcome to the borscht belt."

CHAPTER EIGHT

A Portrait of the Artist as a Young *Tummler,* or, A Widow in the Lobby of Grossinger's Sees a New Fellow. "Excuse Me," She Says to the Older Gentleman, "Have You Been to the Catskills Before?" "No," the Guy Tells Her, "I Just Got Out of Jail After Serving Twenty Years for Murdering My Wife." "So," Says the Widow, "You're Single!"

Jews love talking of the borscht belt, the way Brooklyn people love talking of the Dodgers and southerners adore hearing tales of Stonewall Jackson.

Unfortunately, Stonewall Jackson, the Brooklyn Dodgers, and the borscht belt are all gone. All that's really left of them is lodged in the memories of *alter kockers,* many of whom no longer can remember or care which stories are true and which are bullshit. On such shaky legs are legends like the borscht belt built.

Okay, so what *were* all those Jews on the Eastern Seaboard doing up there in the Catskill Mountains between Memorial and Labor Day? Eating, mostly. Or mating, sometimes. Or complaining about the dinner portions or the evening's entertainment or the fact that they couldn't find a nice dentist for their darling Delores.

Anyway, let's start at the beginning. The Catskill Mountains, ninety miles north of New York City, were a scrabbly rural area when the first Jews wandered into Sullivan County around 1900. Country bumpkin immigrants, they'd arrived in the mountains in search of farm settings like they had back in Russia.

Almost all of these Catskills pioneers were farm peasants from Lithuania who hadn't liked their taste of urban living in New York City. So, they took whatever grubstakes they had north to Sullivan County. There they bought rundown farmhouses and arid land, and tried to grow the potatoes and chickens that had thrived back home in the shtetls near Vilna.

Luckily for the future of American comedy, few of these peasants could hack out a living in the tired Catskills dirt. Indeed, virtually all of the great dynasties of borscht-belt hospitality began with failed Sullivan County farmers.

There was Abraham Brickman, founder of Brickman's Hotel. Max Levinson, founder of the Tamarack Country Club. Louis and Max Kutscher, who invented Kutscher's Hotel. Even Selig and Malke Grossinger, creators of the world-famous resort that was usually just known as "the G," started off their Catskill careers as broke and broken peasants on the verge of foreclosure.

Though their potatoes wouldn't come, the farmers noticed that their relatives down in the city couldn't be stopped. From visiting them, that is. Especially in the summer, when the broil and humidity in Brooklyn or

Queens would convince many a city-bound working-class Jew that maybe *this* was the weekend to pay a visit with that *meshuggener* farmer uncle up in the mountains.

By about 1910, it finally became clear that the immigrant farmers were never going to break even on their farms. By then, more and more began renting out rooms of their rickety houses and barns to the sweltering masses who kept coming up from the city. What the farmers offered guests was nothing fancy and nothing expensive—when Grossinger's opened in 1914, the sole toilet was an outhouse located fifty yards from the dilapidated barn that served as the chalet.

By the time my Swanee Syncopators were booked to play the Swan Lake Inn in the middle 1920s, the Catskills had been transformed. Gone were the dumpy ramshackle weekend rooming houses where guests would get a meager helping of turnips for lunch.

No, it was by now a genuine resort area, of a kind never before seen in America. From now and evermore, the lure of the Catskills would remain the same. Where else could a city-bound Jew get not only clean country air, but food of the kind and portions your mama used to serve you?

Once the first wave of guests got up to the Catskills, however, the original farmers-cum-hoteliers came to a fateful conclusion. The vacationers, it turned out, needed more than food and air. They also needed to be entertained. This was a distasteful conclusion for the owners, because it meant having to hire outside entertainers to keep the guests diverted and happy.

Performers would soon help many borscht-belt resort owners make their fortunes. Still, most of these first-generation American owners couldn't stand us. They just never understood how grown men—men who liked to sleep until 11:00 A.M.!—could choose to make their living telling jokes or singing songs. To these bosses, entertainers were nothing more than *"frei essers"*—free eaters, nuisances that had to be endured.

Still, the owners did take steps to make sure that their performers didn't lollygag. When the Swanee Syncopators arrived at the Swan Lake Inn, for instance, I learned that my duties would only *begin* with leading the band twice a night, seven days a week. Since the joint was small, I was told, I would also have to double as the resort's social director.

Back then, most guests stayed in the mountains for a week. Not counting my time leading the band, my typical schedule for that week would be something like: Sunday—check-in of guests; Monday night—campfire, marshmallow roast; Tuesday night—musical sketches with guests; Wednesday night—vaudeville night; Thursday—burlesque night; Friday—topsy-turvy night, where the guests wait on the staff; Saturday, talent show with guests.

I was, in a word, a *tummler.* In Yiddish, this word means "noise." And that definition, basically, was the actual job description. *Noise.* My charge was to keep people busy and happy and not thinking about how crappy the food or the rooms were at the resort. If the guests are laughing, went the owner's philosophy, then they're not complaining or checking out.

Now this probably doesn't sound like too dignified a

job. Actually, the professional *tummler* is a Jewish tradition that dates back to the Middle Ages. Back then there was a guy named a *badchen* whose job it was to run around at weddings making lots of slapstick noise. It's a sacred commandment to be joyous at weddings, and the *badchen*'s job was to do whatever was necessary to keep everybody giggling.

At the Swan Lake Inn, doing whatever was necessary meant a *tummler* also had to be an emcee, scenic designer, electrician, and sometimes a busboy. After shows, he had to hang around and schmooze up the guests. He had to laugh at the jokes of unfunny men, and dance and flirt with unattractive women. Then there was our most sacred duty—trying to fix up unattached men and women.

Our main currency for all these jobs was the joke. A gag line, it seemed, was most effective when used with guests unhappy with any aspect of their vacation. If a guest complained about the size of his room, for instance, I would give him a recitation of how lousy my own accommodations in this joint were.

"My room's so small it has a three-cent stamp for a rug," I might say.

If they'd heard that one, I'd try: "My room's so small, the mice are hunchbacked."

Or: "You should see my room. I put the key in the door and it breaks the window. When I complained, they gave me a room without a window."

I was actually present at the invention of one of the most famous one-liners of all time. Woody Allen even used this joke in *Annie Hall* to explain his feelings about how awful life is, and yet how it all still ends too soon. Unfortunately, I didn't make this joke up—it came my way from an angry older Jewish woman complaining to me about the fare at the Swan Lake Inn.

"The food here is terrible!" she said to me. "And such small portions!"

A classic. In reply, I simply said, "Madam, the food at the Swan Lake Inn is fit for a king. Here, King! Here, King!"

The point for the *tummler* was to make a quick hit with a funny line or gag, then get out of there quickly. As the great columnist Walter Winchell used to say, "People don't get bored if you change the subject often enough."

I'm quite sure my love of one-liners came from this mountain laboratory. You had to be able to rat-a-tat-tat them out, on all subjects, to all kinds of people, every hour, day or night.

For some reason, a lot of our guests liked to be insulted—albeit gently.

"I'd like to say we're glad you're here," I'd tell a guy. "I'd like to say it."

Or: "last time I saw you, you were in a nightmare."

Or: "I bet you have no more friends than an alarm clock."

Seeing a couple arguing in the lobby, I might break the tension by saying, "Here's a fastidious couple. She's fast, and he's hideous."

Maybe you had to be there. The point was you shticked just to survive.

When it was time to give the one-liners a rest, *tumm-*

lers would engage in elaborate practical jokes that from a half-century's distance sound ridiculous. One of the more obvious stunts was to break into newlyweds' rooms while they were at dinner, fill the grooms' condoms with water, then leave them hanging all over the room. Class, huh?

Other times, we'd break into *everybody's* rooms, and switch the clothes from suite to suite. A woman might find her bra missing, but a pair of boxer shorts in its place. The guests would be forced to mingle and talk with each other in order to get their clothes back, and—*voilà*—sometimes in the mingling there was the beginning of a romance.

Ah, romance. The reason, many think, why the borscht belt existed at all. To the *tummler,* however, matchmaking was not just a charming and cute way to while away a lazy afternoon. Like I said, it was serious business, one of the main reasons why he existed at all. In Yiddish, he was also a *shadchen.* Literally, this word is defined as "matchmaker," but I prefer Shalom Aleichem's definition of a *shadchen* as a "dealer in livestock."

My problem as a matchmaker was one of sheer numbers. On weekdays, you see, when husbands and single men were back in the city working, women outnumbered the guys at most borscht-belt resorts by a margin of four to one.

What this meant for the social staff was that they always had to take great care of the women who never got asked to dance. Though it sounds mean, we called these women "pots."

Moss Hart, for one, never liked dancing again after

serving a lengthy stint as a *tummler.* "For six years," he said, "I danced with nothing but the pots, and that was enough to make me welcome the glorious choice of sitting down for the rest of my life."

The flip side of the pots were the amorous-minded wives whose husbands had left them alone up here while they went back to the city for their work week. Frequently, the husband would tip the *tummler* before leaving the resort every Sunday night. "Here," he'd say, "take care of my wife while I'm away."

Sometimes, at the risk of our jobs, we did.

From a *tummler*'s perspective, the worst thing that could ever happen was for a drop of rain to fall upon his guests. Whenever it rained, you see, the patrons would tramp back into the main lodge to angrily bray and complain all the way until the next meal.

This was my audience. Talk about working a rough room. But to learn how to make these tough, smart, no-bullshit vacationers from the city laugh was the best comedy trade school a guy could have wanted.

Just look at a partial list of borscht-belt *tummlers* who made it to the big time: Danny Kaye, Jan Peerce, Jan Murray, Tony Curtis, Jerry Lewis, Red Buttons, Phil Silvers, Moss Hart, Jack Albertson, Joey Adams, Jack Carter, and Phil Foster. There are many more, but I'm not big on list-making.

Of course, *tummling* was never glamorous—Alan King's quarters while working at the White Roe Inn consisted of a fold-up cot onstage. Nor was it ever financially rewarding—most *tummlers* lived for that tip at the end of a guest's stay.

(By the way, Red Buttons came up with the cleverest

idea for supplementing his meager salary. Borscht-belt dining halls, of course, were strictly kosher—no mixing meat and milk allowed. Still, a lot of younger guests wanted cream in their coffee. Red's trick was to fill up a fountain pen with cream, make the table rounds at dinner, and give a squirt to whoever didn't want their coffee black. The charge was twenty-five cents a *shpritz*.)

Despite the meager rewards of *tummling,* the borscht belt gave me an education not available in any ivory-towered academy. For one thing, I learned the all-important meaning of going-too-far. Take what I did on one of those fateful Catskills days when it rained and the masses came into the lobby as ornery as a pack of hungry jackals. On this particular evening, the schedule had promised them a big campfire, marshmallow roast, and folk-song fest.

The guests, cheated out of their chance to be one with nature, took out their complaints on me. "All right," I finally told them, "you want a campfire, I'll build you a campfire."

And so I did. Right in the middle of the lobby. My plan was to build a little fire, stamp it out, get a couple of yuks. What I got, however, was a blaze big enough to necessitate the arrival of several local volunteer fire departments.

Still, not all Catskills trade in those days involved shoveling shtick and *kishka* into vacationing Jews. There was, for example, a burgeoning bootleg-booze industry. It began while Prohibition was on during the twenties, when local farmers began cooking up huge batches of pungent whiskey called "Catskills Applejack."

This industry brought the first hoods to the borscht

belt; the bootleggers were joined in the thirties by some of the biggest all-around gangsters around. It seemed that the rocky and still largely uncharted Catskills provided perfect hideouts for lamsters on the run, or for gangsters in need of some rest and relaxation.

And so the crooks came. One of the most famous was Legs Diamond, the charming killer who later owned the always-hopping Hotsy Totsy Club in Manhattan. Then there was Dutch Schultz, the completely *meshuggener* bootlegger and murderer who was as hot-blooded as Legs was cool. Completing the rogues' trifecta was Vincent "Mad Dog" Coll, Dutch's former number-one hit man. Not only did Dutch not give Mad Dog a good job reference—he eventually had him whacked.

The two Catskills cultures—the kibbitzing Jews and the blustery gangsters—rarely intersected. My own scariest run-in with the Catskills goodfellas came during my second summer at the Swan Lake Inn.

The encounter came about because of a surefire scheme my cousin Jimmy and I had hit on to supplement our minuscule *tummler's* salaries. First, we would buy huge volumes of punchboards, those little penny-ante gambling games that one could buy by mail from the ads in the back of *Variety*. Then, we would peddle them on our off-hours to hotels and drugstores in the Catskills. Easy, we figured.

It was, until, a member of Dutch Schultz's gang of happy goons intercepted us on our second day of business. This fellow's face looked as if it had met the wrong end of a waffle iron, but we were impressed by his very persuasive presentation. No, sir, we told him, we had no idea that Mr. Schultz controlled all matters relating to gambling in these parts. Yes, sir, thank you sir, we said, promising to never push another punchboard for the duration of our lives.

It's amazing to me how some of these gangsters are now considered folk heroes and men of the people. Let me tell you, these fellows were playing for real, and they didn't shoot blanks.

There was, for example, an even more bizarre intersection between the hoods and the Jewish resort community. It happened on a summer morning, as a body was discovered in Swan Lake, just off the Swan Lake Inn. No, our staff quickly ascertained, the unfortunate victim wasn't a guest.

Whoever it was, was a dapper-suited gentleman wearing something large and metallic around his neck. The police later ascertained that the guy was a proprietor of one of Legs Diamond's local gambling joints. It seems the fellow had gotten a little greedy, and had given Legs the receipts from only ten of the joint's eleven slot machines. The profits from machine number eleven he kept for himself.

Legs found out he was being skimmed, and his wayward employee was given a quick trip to the bottom of Swan Lake. Before the guy was tossed in, however, Legs directed that the hood be fitted with an anchor a little more creative in styling than simple cement slippers. And that's why the local police found the guy at the bottom of the lake wearing slot machine number eleven around his neck.

As you can see, I learned lessons in the Catskills far

beyond mere *tummling* and timing. I also learned of hustlers, gangsters, con men, and honor among thieves. Believe you me, these are good things to know about if you're planning on entering show business in any capacity.

Anyway, the sheer volume of gags I had to generate while *tummling* in the borscht belt left me forever joke-poor. The problem intensified when I decided to come back several more summers. Because most of the hotels' business were repeaters, I couldn't just tell the same old stuff I'd done the year before. For a *tummler* in this kind of distress, there was, thankfully, a black market in jokes.

This thriving industry operated out of three establishments in midtown Manhattan where platoons of comics—stars, would-bes, never-weres, and has-beens—hung out and *shpritzed.* For a price, or for a swap in kind, stolen routines could be had in Kellogg's Cafeteria on Forty-ninth Street and Seventh Avenue, the Theatrical Drugstore on Forty-sixth, or the Palace Cafeteria west of Sixth Avenue.

There, a *tummler* could barter two Milton Berle routines, say, for a George Jessel toastmaster introduction. Once in a while I bought, but usually I traded. Occasionally, I even had enough material that I could afford to sell some stuff.

One of the guys whom I made a deal with was a pretty well known older comic named Buddy Walker. Walker had been around a while and had had some success. Now, however, his routine was getting stale—I don't think he'd inserted a new joke into his routine since McKinley was president.

To this day, I can still remember Buddy Walker's trademark joke. He'd walk onstage with a cat, and tell the crowd that "I stole this cat from a guy who runs a poker game in the Leamington Hotel. I heard someone say there was fifty dollars in the kitty." Ugh. A *putz*.

Anyway, I run into Walker one day in one of the comic cafeterias. I'm there to scrounge up some more material for the Catskills; Walker is there to scrounge up an act. He told me he'd give me fifty bucks that afternoon for whatever spare material I had.

At the set hour, I waited for Mr. Walker in front of the Lobster restaurant on Forty-fifth Street. Right on time, Buddy pulls up in a fancy-shmancy Stutz Bearcat. He hops out, and gives me one of the biggest brush-offs I'd ever gotten in my life.

"Bastard!" I yelled, remembering that great mob lesson about how to deal with a lack of respect: Don't get mad, get even. It's a stupid rule, of course, a rule for idiots. But I was young, remember. And Buddy Walker had just played me for a chump, leaving a trail of attitude as he stomped past me to meet his big-shot cronies inside the famous Dinty Moore Restaurant.

Left outside the restaurant, I considered my options. I had fifty cents in my pocket, and a heart bent on revenge. Suddenly, I noticed that to the left of me a sign painter's truck was parked in front of a little tailor's shop. When I approached, the painters were splashing up an advertisement that said something about refastening zippers for thirty-five cents.

Pointing to Buddy Walker's Stutz Bearcat, I told the painters that I was broke and needed to sell my car. I told them I'd give them my last half a buck if they would paint "For Sale—$25" on the side of the car. They nodded yes, and I watched in pleasure as they wrote the message large over Buddy Walker's beloved roadster.

In time, Buddy came out of the restaurant and saw what I had done. We encountered each other often over the years, but Buddy Walker never spoke to me again.

Putz.

After my little encounter with the brush-off artist, I headed back to the borscht belt with my newly bartered-for selection of *tummler* material. It's important to point out, however, that just memorizing some new gags was the simplest part of the job. The hard part was working out timing, topicality, and rapport with the guests. In the borscht belt, you had to quickly develop an instinct for saying the exact right thing at the exact right moment.

Today, young comics have an entire network of cross-country clubs in which to hone their acts and practice their crafts. In my day, there was nowhere to go but the Catskills. It still fills me with awe that an entire institution like the borscht belt can be born, flower, flourish, and die in the span of one man's lifetime.

And then it was gone. I happen to have been staying at Grossinger's in time to see the death rattle. It must have been the summer of 1984, and the grand old "G" was making a last-ditch attempt to stay alive by luring in younger hepcats.

The weekend I was there, Grossinger's hosted a "fifteenth anniversary of Woodstock reunion." That big rock concert, of course, occurred only a few miles from the resort. A lot of those big hoo-ha rock stars actually got to the Woodstock stage in 1969 by taking helicopters from Grossinger's front lawn.

Anyway, the G hosts this reunion, and brings in a bunch of over-the-hill rock bands to entertain the masses of boys and girls who they expected would beat down the resort's doors to be a part of such a celebration.

The problem was that nobody but the press showed up. Abbie Hoffman was there, giving interviews out in the Eddie Cantor Room, but no kids.

I still remember going to the Grossinger's auditorium that night, where I was blasted out by the loudest, worst music I ever heard in my life. The *bubbes* were running out of there holding their ears, wondering what had happened to their beloved Grossinger's.

What had happened was that the Catskills party was finally over.

What had happened can perhaps be best found in *Dirty Dancing,* that hit movie with Joel Grey's daughter about wiggling your tush in the getting-ready-to-die borscht belt.

There's a scene in the movie in which Max Kellerman, the owner of the fictional Kellerman Resort, is reminiscing about the old days in the borscht belt. "*Bubbe* and *Zayde* serving the first pasteurized milk to the boarders . . . through the war years, when we didn't have any meat . . . through the Depression, when we didn't have anything."

At this point, Kellerman's bandleader chips in, "Lots of changes, Max. Lots of changes."

With that, Max sums it all up nicely. "It isn't the

changes so much," he says. "It's that it all seems to be ending. You think kids want to come with their parents to take fox-trot lessons? Trips to Europe, that's what the kids want. Twenty-two countries in three days."

Max pauses. "Seems like it's all slipping away."

Sadly, in the end, the borscht belt did just that.

CHAPTER NINE

Speakeasies and Gangsters, or, I Used to Play This Place in Paterson, New Jersey, Called the Lido Venice. This Place Was So Tough the Hatcheck Girl's Name Was Rocco.

At the end of my first summer in the borscht belt, I returned to New York bearing no better prospects than when I'd left. My skills remained spotty. I could *tummel*. I could lead a rinky-dink band. I could come back with an ad-lib pretty good.

I did not have what you'd call great expectations.

Still, I continued to diligently scrounge around town for gigs for the Swanee Syncopators. But my bread and butter remained those unglamorous printing skills that had been drummed into my head and fingers at Brooklyn Vocational High School.

Indeed, by now those talents had grown far beyond

my duties as a flunky in the printing booth in Kresge's Department Store basement. Or so my father told me.

Pa, convinced I was the next Gutenberg, somehow borrowed a couple of hundred dollars and bought me a small Atkinson press. We schlepped it down to the basement of our tenement, and I set up shop as a self-employed inkstained wretch.

Now, my days were mostly filled with nights. Many evenings began with a Swanee Syncopators gig. After our sojourn in the Catskills, the group started adding more and more comedy numbers to our song list. But we were willing to play any style for a buck, at times even turning into what they used to call a "society orchestra." You know, the kind of band that would play in tuxes at museums for the benefit of dancing dowagers. In these situations, believe it or not, we went by the handle "Henny Youngman and His Society Kings."

After a band gig, I would begin my second career. As midnight came and went, I would take the subway from wherever I was to the downtown Brooklyn theater district. There, I would go around to all of the late-night restaurants and stir up printing business from the actors and musicians in residence.

I offered prospective clients a not-bad deal. With me, a performer could lay down a buck and get two hundred business cards detailing all his particulars from name and phone number all the way down to his instrument. Among the extras I offered my customers was *almost*-instant delivery.

I worked it like this. After I had snared a couple of business-card orders, I would hustle back by subway to my folks' Bay Ridge apartment and the Atkinson press. I would print up the new cards as fast as I could, then speed back downtown to deliver the goods—usually before the performers had finished their last cups of coffee.

By now, I'd be so spent from my evening labors that I often couldn't face one last and long subway trip home. Instead, I'd often walk up the steps to Sadie's nearby tenement at about three or four in the morning, and bang on the door for admittance.

Though Sadie's ma definitely didn't approve of my lifestyle, she often allowed me to sack out on the couch in their living room. I was not, needless to say, the prince she had been hoping would come along and save Sadie from her life pushing sheet music in the Kresge's basement.

BUM, Sadie's ma's eyes still said.

But what could I do? I am what I am, and I was what I was. I was, of course, busting my chops trying to make a living between the band and the printing. I didn't *want* to be working these graveyard-shift hours, I explained to Sadie and her mother. But that's when and where the work was for a man of my catholic talents.

Still, I had my eyes set on bigger things for me and my little Atkinson printing press. Soliciting business-card orders from actors and musicians working the downtown Brooklyn theater district wasn't bad. But I figured I could probably double my scores by moving my press to the land where show-biz people congregated in lemminglike numbers.

Sadie, my million-dollar baby, I told my beloved, I'm moving my printing business from my folks' basement to

Manhattan. I was ready to make the jump from Brooklyn to Broadway. "Good for you, Hen," said Sadie, who was never one for melodramatics. Her ma wasn't too happy about it though—especially when I told her I would still be returning to Brooklyn from Manhattan late every evening. Her couch, it seemed, would still not yet be safe from me.

And so, granted these tepid blessings, I went ahead and rented a tiny printing booth of my own in a penny arcade on Sixth Avenue between Forty-fifth and Forty-sixth streets. Now, I was within crawling distance of virtually every big theater in town.

I had arrived in printing heaven. For wherever there were theaters, I figured, there were also actors. And wherever there were actors, there were also out-of-work actors, hustling agents, and small armies of the type of professionals who constantly need rush printing orders on the quick and cheap.

For advertising, I draped a large piece of cardboard over the front of my stand that read; HENNY YOUNGMAN—PRINCE OF PRINTERS. For product, I offered the same kind of crap that I did back in Brooklyn. Business cards for show-business people. Letterheads for shady businesses. And "fun cards" for people who wouldn't mind putting out ten cents for ten jokes like:

1. Didn't I see your picture on an iodine bottle?

Or:

2. I had a date with a Siamese twin, but she couldn't get away.

Or:

3. Do you mind if I smoke? I don't mind if you burn.

I'll spare you the rest. For now.

I even began advertising myself. Any client who allowed me to print "Henny Youngman—Funny Violinist" on the back of a business card got half off. Yes, I had gone from thinking of myself as just plain old fiddle player to a guy who did funny things with his band.

It seemed like a natural progression. Like I said, I'd been adding more and more comedy songs to the Swanee Syncopators' repertoire ever since we returned from our first engagement in the Catskills.

But as with most momentous things in my life, my transition from musician to stand-up comedian came about as a total mistake. The lightning struck while the Swanee Syncopators were in the middle of a two-week engagement at a joint called the Nut Club in Pinedale, New Jersey. We were the bottom of the bill, the headliners being the pretty damn good dance team of Grace and Paul Hartman. Maybe you've heard of their son David, the guy who was on *Good Morning America.*

One Saturday night, for reasons I never found out, the Hartmans didn't show up. I found this out when a frantic Ed Ball, the Nut Club's manager, rushed into our band's dressing room—a broom closet with a hook.

"Henny," Ed said, "you've got to go on for the Hartmans tonight. Solo. Stand-up. You've got to save my life."

Ed had apparently seen me cutting up with the band in rehearsal. Now, with a Saturday night crowd flowing in and no headline act, he had to improvise with the only thing he had. Me.

It worked.

I got lucky that night. A big party came in and loved my routine, which was just a random assemblage of bits I had picked up over my years of hanging out on the fringes of the show-biz community. After the show, Ed Ball came up and threw his arms around me.

"Who needs a band?" he told me. "Henny, all you need is *you*. Do you want to be my house comedian for the next two weeks?"

I thought the offer over for two, maybe three, seconds. Just think—I wouldn't have to schlep instruments and other people around. I could be responsible for just myself. I would get paid just as much for working alone as I was getting to head the Syncopators. "Yeah," I said, shaking Phil's hand, "I'll do it."

And so, whither the Swanee Syncopators. When Harry Ritz heard the news that I'd given up the band for standup, he said simply, "Music's loss is comedy's loss."

Maybe so. But not even a two-week gig could free me from the daily twelve-hour grind at the penny-arcade printing booth. To pass my never-ending shift inside the booth, I kept up a daylong comic patter with whoever walked by.

As the characters of midtown Manhattan perused my printing goods, I would do a little spiel, tell the latest jokes, cook up any shtick that would break the tedium of busting your ass for a living. One day, a young guy who looked as if he was in an awful hurry walked past my booth. I tossed him a gag, and the fellow pulled up short, and wheeled on me.

"That's my joke," the guy told me. Even before he'd spoken a word, however, I recognized the guy. It was Milton Berle, two years younger than I was, but already famous. A legitimate big shot.

At that moment, Milton was the featured headliner at Loews State, a classy theater a couple of blocks over on Broadway. Milton was doing six shows a day there, and whenever he had a little break, he would go for a walk around the neighborhood. That's how he happened to be tramping by my booth.

Now, after seeing the ad in my booth for printed "fun cards," he even laid down a dime for ten of my fossilized jokes.

"These stink!" Milton said, skimming through the gags.

"I know," I said, pocketing his ten cents.

We schmoozed for a while, tossing jokes back and forth to each other like the dueling banjoists in *Deliverance.* Milton liked me, I liked him, and he invited me over to see his show at Loews. I went, time and again, to see the show and then go backstage and *shpritz* with Milton about the craft of comedy.

Milton and I were pals; we didn't have a teacher-student relationship. He didn't even try to tamper with my fast style of delivery. He saw that that rhythm was *me*—and that nothing else would work.

Still, I would have had to have been a complete dope not to listen to Milton's thoughts on comedy. He'd made his Broadway comic debut in 1920 at age twelve in *Floradora,* and he knew everything about show biz. If you ever forgot that Milton knew everything, he'd remind you.

Very soon, Milton began throwing me stand-up gigs that he'd turned down. By then, he thought he was beyond performing bar mitzvahs and small clubs. I, needless to say, was more than grateful for any exposure and any paying gig.

(By the way, and nothing against Milton, but I've never thought I was too big for a bar mitzvah. I still remember this night a few years ago when I had just finished playing this big date at New York's Waldorf Astoria. The adrenaline had pumped for that performance—I was getting top dollar that evening to play before sixty-five-hundred people. Anyway, I finish the date, and board the Waldorf elevator for the ride down to the lobby. By mistake, however, I get off at the second floor. Standing there is a hotel bulletin board that says LEVY BAR MITZVAH, ROOM 240. I go to room 240, ask for Mr. Levy, introduce myself, and ask if he'd like me to do ten or fifteen minutes for the party. He did, and I made an extra $150. Ah, what a night!)

Anyway, between the good word of mouth about my brand-new comedy act at the Nut Club in New Jersey and Milton's referrals, I started to get regular bookings. Not enough to live on yet, not enough so I could go and ask for Sadie's hand, but enough so that I could daydream about the day when I could retire that goddam Atkinson printing press.

Since Prohibition was still on, virtually all of the New York nightclubs where comics could find work were located in illegal speakeasies. Some of them were classy, with the classiest all seeming to be on Fifty-second Street. The fanciest, most exclusive of all the speaks was "21"—yes, the same "21" as today. The prices in there were

"This is me as a little kid, to the left of my brother, Lester. Notice the resemblance between me at seven and Isaac Bashevis Singer at eighty-three?"

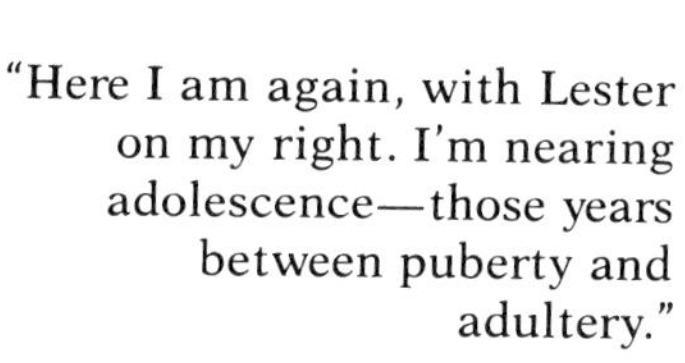

"Here I am again, with Lester on my right. I'm nearing adolescence—those years between puberty and adultery."

"A portrait of the artist as a young *meshugganeh*. I'm about seventeen here, wearing the trademark smirk of an underachieving class clown."

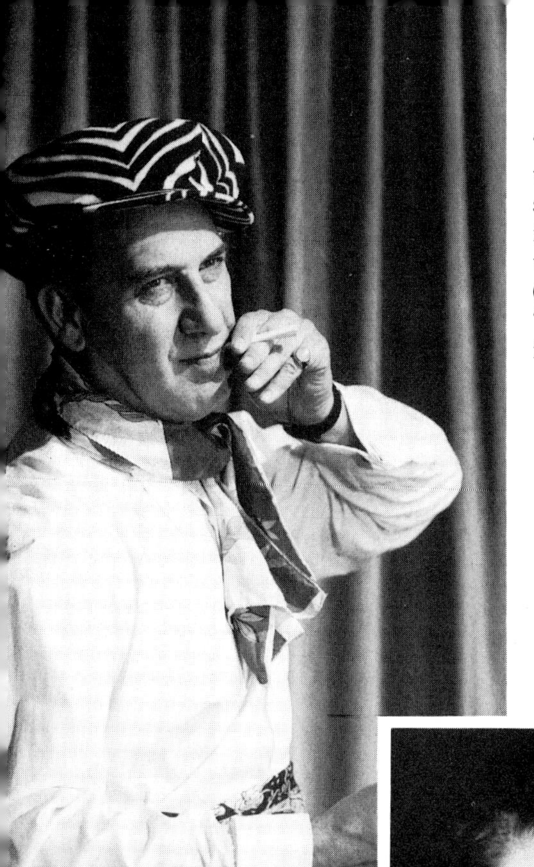

"I can't remember what this was a photograph of, but I'm sure it was something interesting. I know I'm wearing someone else's hat (Joey Heatherton's?). As I said, 'If you want dignity, don't go into show biz.' "

"Here I am with Marilyn, kid number one, at age ten. Marilyn is my million-dollar baby . . . before taxes."

"Here I am in the 1960s, trying to keep the peace between the two most famous noses in comedy—Mr. Hope and Mr. Durante."

ZINN ARTHUR

"I get a surprise birthday party in the 1940s, courtesy of Marilyn, number-one son, Gary, and Sadie. We weren't exactly the Ozzie and Harriet Nelson family, but the Youngmans of Bay Ridge, Brooklyn, had our share of fun."

"Me futzing around with Jack Benny in 1970. Jack always claimed he was a worse violinist than me; I always disagreed. He was bad . . . but I was terrible." ZINN ARTHUR

"Here's Marilyn, Sadie, Gary, my ma, and me at the opening of Club Carmen in New Jersey. I still remember Ma's disbelieving words when I showed her my first check for telling jokes: 'Since when were you funny?' "

"Here's the family at Marilyn's sweet sixteen. She's a doll, ain't she? And Gary—the best. Sadie, of course, was the unbeatable *Sadie*. And me? I was making a living."

"Sadie and me not long before the end of our fifty-six-year partnership. After she got sick, she insisted I keep telling the wife jokes. Anyway, Sadie and I had a great run together . . . and I miss her every second of every day." ZINN ARTHUR

"You think Mort Sahl is the only comic who finds jokes in the headlines? Here's what I came up with this particular day while winging my way to Minneapolis: Imelda Marcos was so happy to have been acquitted that she immediately flew to Israel to plant a shoe tree." ZINN ARTHUR unbelievable for the day—a cocktail cost a buck, and champagne went for twenty-five dollars.

Customers could relax in "21"'s two bars or restaurants, on the massive dance floor, or in one of the several lounges outfitted with couches, Ping-Pong tables and backgammon sets. Even mah-jongg, then a very hip game, was available. And what if the cops should raid? No problem. Entire sections of wall holding incriminating evidence could disappear, replaced by revolving hidden shelves.

"21" was the high end of the speakeasy social scale on Fifty-second Street. The low end was several yards away, at a speak known as "the International Hair Net Manufacturers' Association."

The place consisted of one tiny room, on whose west wall someone had hung a framed hair net. In the middle of the room was a battered desk, and a safe. Inside the safe were a couple of shot glasses and some mason jars filled with the world's worst rotgut whiskey. Well, what do you expect from a bar that bills itself "the International Hair Net Manufacturers' Association"?

By the time I arrived on the scene as a hopeful comic, there were probably around seventy of these illegal nightclubs in New York. All of these speakeasies had a few things in common. All had scantily clad cigarette girls running around selling smokes for a dollar a pack. They also had contingents of girls hawking five-dollar Kewpie dolls. "Hey, mister," the vendors would say, "a Kewpie for your cutie?"

To not buy a Kewpie for your date was considered highly chintzy. Customers were also expected to throw in a sizable tip—usually you just doubled the price.

Besides having revolving walls, there were several ways speakeasies managed to thwart the cops and stay open. One common ploy was to *not* actually serve booze. Instead, skittish barkeeps learned, you could do a hefty business selling "setups."

The routine was this. Men would bring hip flasks in their pockets, while women would smuggle in whole bottles of bootleg booze under their coats. After being seated, they could purchase their setup. Ginger ale went for $1.50 a glass, and a pitcher of tap water could be had for only $20.

Rye—if the speakeasy carried it—usually cost around ten bucks a bottle. There was also a new invention around town called either a "cover charge" or "*couvert* charge"—and it sometimes ran up to twenty dollars at some of the fancier speaks.

A great number of these nightclubs, of course, were owned and run by gangsters. A lot of these characters, you see, wanted to be taken seriously by high society. The quickest way to social acceptability, they figured, was to open a swanky club and play toastmaster to the swells.

And hoo-boy, everybody *did* mix.

One of the first gangsters to jump into the club scene was Owney Madden. In the old days, Madden had been the leader of the notorious Gopher Gang from Manhattan's Hell's Kitchen. Later, he was one of the biggest bootleggers in town.

As Prohibition carried on, Madden also began picking up pieces of some of the very hottest clubs in town. Besides the Cotton Club, Madden also had a popular place called the Silver Slipper on Forty-eighth Street, which featured a nutty comedy trio called Clayton, Jackson, and Durante. That's young Jimmy Durante, for those who don't remember.

Then there was the gangster Larry Fay, a rumrunner from Hell's Kitchen who bankrolled several clubs run by the famous and gorgeous Texas Guinan, the empress of New York nightlife whose alternate nickname was "the Queen of Whoopee." Among Fay and Guinan's clubs were the El Fay, Intime, the Three Hundred Club, and Texas Guinan's.

At each of her clubs, the ever-glamorous Texas would sit in the middle of the *mishegoss,* waving her diamonds, blowing a police whistle to encourage bedlam, and convincing proper elderly millionaires to go down to the dance floor and play leapfrog.

Her customary greeting to all customers was "Hello, sucker." Her usual way of applauding some dignified young woman who'd just done something drunk or scandalous in the club was "Give this little girl a great big hand!" The dough may have been Larry Fay's, but the star was definitely Texas Guinan.

Dutch Schultz, meantime, had a fancy-shmancy place called the Embassy Club on East Fifty-seventh Street. That's where Helen Morgan basically invented the art form of torch singing. Sitting on a piano, Morgan would just keep belting out tearjerkers like "Bill."

This is the world in which I worked. And soon after I started working the speakeasies, I had more close-up looks at some of the underworld kingpins and the way they did business.

Milton knew a lot of these gangsters, and he recommended me to the management of a classy speakeasy called the Club Abbey, which was located on the first floor of a West Fifty-fourth Street brownstone. I went over big my first night there, and the goons who ran the joint signed me up for a nice run.

Club Abbey drew an amazingly diverse crowd. On one typical night, I might see actress Beatrice Lillie sitting next to a table headed by gangster Arnold "the Big Bankroll" Rothstein, who in turn was perched a few feet away from New York mayor Jimmy Walker. Crazy days.

And nights. And now, sixty years later, I have no trouble remembering the craziest night of all. It came in the middle of what I now believed was going to be a long and fruitful engagement at Club Abbey.

Beginning my act one night, I noticed the usual crowd of swells and dandified tough guys at the front tables. I could see that Milton Berle had showed up after his own performance in town that night to see me perform—we both tried to catch each other's acts as often as possible.

Up front I also saw Larry Fay, along with Dutch Schultz, Martin "the Crumpet" Krompier, and Chink Sherman, who it turned out was on the run from the Boston cops. Like Schultz, Chink led a massive bootleg gang—and the two men were bitter enemies. I wasn't too nervous at the sight of all this muscle, however. For also up front near these prominent characters, I saw equally prominent New York Police chief detective John J. Walsh. No reason to worry, right?

Wrong. By this time in my career, my act was evolving from me telling monologues to me doing just one-liners. I was in a middle phase that night at Club Abbey, doing what would probably now be called "insult humor."

You know, Don Rickles–type stuff, in the years before Don Rickles had to comb his hair with a towel.

It was amazing how much the gangsters loved this kind of humor, which seems pretty restrained when compared to the insults comics throw around onstage now. Back then, though, it was considered pretty rough material. Stuff like:

> Someday you'll go far, and I hope you stay there.

Or:

> There's a train leaving in half an hour. Be under it!

Or:

> I looked high and low for you. I didn't look low enough.

You get the idea. Anyway, the tough guys loved me talking this way to them from the stage. They'd always invite me to sit with them after the show, where I'd continue to amaze them by the simple fact that I didn't drink. They couldn't believe it. I didn't tell them I had a bad stomach—it would ruin my mystique. Anyway, the gangsters liked me. They wanted me around.

So, I wasn't too worried to see this little convention of hoods in front of me that night at Club Abbey. Except, as my act went on, the insults started coming faster from the gangsters than from me.

Soon after I'd begun, Chink Sherman hurled an epithet at Dutch Schultz, his nearby blood enemy. A very drunk Dutch, never one to back down from an insult, unleashed a stream of invective of his own at Chink. Plodding ahead with my act as best as I could, I noticed that Police Detective Walsh had bolted from his table and was headed for an exit.

And then the lights went out. There were gunshots, many of them. There were screams, and the crashes of bottles and tables being overturned. When the lights came back on, Club Abbey was trashed.

Chink Sherman was lying over by the stage, where he'd been shot twice, stabbed, and beaten over the head with a chair. Dutch, a few feet away, had multiple stab wounds and a bullet in his shoulder. Unbelievably, they both survived.

For a while, anyway—both men would die of not-very-natural causes in the next few years. Milton and I, however, did not stick around the Club Abbey long enough to get the box score of the incident. Jumping off the stage, I joined my pal in running out the door.

As we sprinted down Fifty-fourth Street, sirens coming nearer us and Club Abbey, I yelled to Milton. "Ah," I said, "show business!"

"Nothing like it," Milton agreed, as we rushed toward Broadway.

While my engagement at Club Abbey may have ended—the cops shuttered the place for good the morning after the shootings—I was not yet nearly done with gangsters.

New Jersey, of course, was just as fertile territory for hoods as New York. After my successful debut at the Nut

Club in Pinedale, I got several more bookings in Jersey nightclubs. Almost every single club, it turned out, was controlled by a mobster.

Of those clubs, the roughest and toughest was a place called the Lido Venice, located in beautiful downtown Paterson, New Jersey. To this day, I make reference to the Lido Venice in virtually every single club act I perform.

"This club the Lido Venice was so tough," I spiel, "that the hatcheck's girl's name was Rocco."

And: "This club the Lido Venice was so tough," I'd go on, "that the boss used to *stab* me good night."

And on and on, all at the Lido Venice—a joint whose specialty was gangster-brewed applejack and comics who could make the tough guys laugh. Which I always could. For reasons I still don't understand. All I understood back then was that if the gangsters liked you, they'd often throw you a fifty at the end of the night to show their appreciation.

Anyway, one night I'm sitting at a table about an hour before I go on at the Lido Venice. A couple of characters whom I know well enough to nod to come up and say hello, how are you, we enjoyed your show last night, that kind of stuff.

The first is Abner "Longy Zwillman," a dapper tough guy who went from Meyer Lansky and Bugsy Siegel's gang in Brooklyn to being one of the biggest bootleggers in the East. After Dutch Schultz got hit while taking a leak in the Palace Chophouse in Newark, Longy became the boss of the New Jersey rackets.

Along with Longy that night was a less refined hood named Waxey Gordon. Waxey had started off in the mob as a *shlammer,* a breaker of bones and heads. He rose in the ranks until he hit his prime as a bootlegger. Longy took a liking to his young rival Waxey, even going so far as to teach him one of the most famous Zwillman secrets of bootlegging.

The problem for all bootleggers, you see, was how to move beer from an illegal brewery or warehouse without the cops knowing about it. Longy's genius solution, which Waxey expanded and perfected, was to utilize a city's own sewer pipes to move beer.

The trick was to tape up mobile clay pipes in the sewer in the middle of the night. Before morning, Waxey's beer would have flowed from the brewery, through the pipes in the sewer, all the way to a pickup point at the other end of town. There, tank trucks could leisurely tap into the pipes and begin their deliveries to outlying areas.

Waxey's genius was for distribution, not good manners. Indeed, that night when he and Longy sat and chewed the fat at my table at the Club Lido, I saw something that blew any notions I might ever have had that these gangsters were glamorous.

While we are all bullshitting, this pretty Jewish waitress walks past Waxey with her drink tray. Waxey, it turned out, had been watching her for a couple of days, had even made a couple of unsuccessful advances. Seeing her again, he pulled something out from under his dinner jacket and motioned for me to reach for it under the table.

"Listen, kid," he said. "I want you to do me a favor. Hold this till I get back. There's a waitress in this place who has something I want."

Under the table I took hold of Waxey's personal automatic pistol. I could barely lift it; as I shoved it down my pants, I watched as Waxey nonchalantly walked out toward the kitchen.

He returned several minutes later looking none the worse for wear. I gave him back his heater, and he winked and slid a C-note into my vest pocket. "She's a nice girl. You did a nice job, Henny. Have a drink."

I reexplained to Waxey that I didn't drink. Waxey shook his head, throwing me that befuddled look that gangsters get when confronted by something they don't understand, like comics who don't drink.

"Okay, kid, enjoy," Waxey said, heading out the front door, a satisfied man.

Curious about what had gone on, I headed back through the kitchen and out the back exit. There, on the ground, was the pretty waitress. No, she hadn't wanted to give Waxey what he'd wanted. So he punched her in the mouth, breaking her jaw. Then he ripped her dress, and raped her.

She was crying softly, making a tiny sound that sounded worse to me than wailing. After a few minutes, I walked her down to a mob doctor who lived a couple doors down from the club. Before leaving the doc's, I took him aside and pressed Waxey's hundred-dollar bill into his hand and asked him to make her well.

He promised, and I headed out the door, back to the club, feeling like a heel. I went on that night at the Club Lido, but I have no idea how I did.

All I knew, heading back to Brooklyn after the show, was what I'd figured out seeing that poor pretty woman, hurt and all alone.

It was probably four in the morning when I finally got back to downtown Brooklyn. I walked up to Chauncey

Street, banged on the door of Sadie's family's apartment, and waited for that BUM look from Sadie's ma.

It came. But, as always, Mrs. Cohen motioned for me to help myself to the couch.

But tonight, I didn't want to sleep—I wanted Sadie.

Running up the stairs, Mrs. Cohen two feet behind me threatening to call the police, I entered Sadie's room.

"Marry me, Sadie, please, I love you," I said.

She said yes.

Little did either of us know that our match wouldn't end for over half a century. In the coming years, I would make an industry out of making fun of my wife onstage. But not once did I ever regret frantically running up those stairs on Chauncey Street in search of my Sadie's hand.

We had a great run.

CHAPTER TEN

From Vaudeville Whorehouses to the Back Booth at Lindy's, or, Even If Walter Winchell Calls You "the King of One-Liners," You're Still a Bum to Your Mother-in-Law

My prospects still seemed dim when Sadie and I were married in a tiny ceremony in Brooklyn in 1928. Even with my dual careers as comic and printer, I was still an intimate acquaintance of poverty. Hence, it only made sense for Sadie and me—us!—to move in with her mother on Chauncey Street.

Oops.

Now, even at this late date in the century, I can honestly say that I had nothing personal against Mrs. Cohen, my new mother-in-law. True, she never did really forgive me for being neither Yehudi Menuhin nor Albert Einstein. Actually, she figured, her daughter Sadie deserved a husband who was *both* Yehudi Menuhin and Albert Einstein.

Anyway, my feelings for Mrs. Cohen notwithstanding, I would like to point out that it wasn't I who invented the mother-in-law joke. I merely perfected it.

Indeed, making fun of your mother-in-law has been a staple of traditional Jewish humor for centuries. The insults probably originated from a commonplace occurrence in Jewish life of the old days—sons-in-law being supported for a few years after the marriage by the bride's parents.

Though I was paying my new family's way, I was still living in my mother-in-law's house. Let me tell you, this kind of overfamiliarity will most definitely breed a strain of contempt. As Shalom Aleichem himself once said, "Adam was the luckiest man to ever live, because he had no mother-in-law."

And why are mother-in-law jokes so funny, even in this day and age of quite proper feminist sensitivities? How the hell should I know? Still, I do get a kick out of these scholarly types who've tried to figure out to the comma what makes things like mother-in-law jokes tick.

Here, in front of me, I've got a learned book on comedy written by a very serious and smart-looking guy with a Ph.D. in sociology from the New School for Social Research in New York City. Mr. Big Shot.

Anyway, let me quote, if you don't mind, from a chapter the professor has written entitled "On Method":

"Such a relationship becomes clear if one refers to such a standard comic convention as the mother-in-law joke. The comedy grows out of the specific relationship of tension between mother-in-law and son-in-law. The mother-in-law joke would be no joke if the comedy were made to derive from some random quirk of the mother-in-law heroine that had nothing to do with that relationship."

Excuse me, Professor, are you through with your ridiculous sermon? Because I have absolutely no idea what you're talking about. You want to know why mother-in-law jokes are funny? Here. I'll show you.

"I just got back from a pleasure trip. I drove my mother-in-law to the airport."

Or:

"My mother-in-law is so nearsighted that she nagged a coat hanger for an hour."

Or:

"My mother-in-law rarely goes without saying."

There. *These* are why mother-in-law jokes are funny. Anyway, as I was saying, I really *did* like Mrs. Cohen. Still, things were getting a little tight on Chauncey Street, and I thought it best if Sadie and I got our own place. "Fine," said Sadie. "Fine," said Mrs. Cohen.

"Fine," said the landlady as I counted out nine dollars, our first week's rent at the tiny cold-water one-room flat I'd just let. Unfortunately, this was all I could afford to spend on rent for me and my new wife. Sadie wasn't exactly enthused about the notion of living in a shoebox, but she understood.

What she didn't quite comprehend was why she had to live the first several months in our shoebox *alone.* Looking back, I guess it wasn't good timing to tell Sadie eight days after we were married that I had to leave New York to hit the vaudeville provinces.

I tried to explain to her that vaudeville bookers don't care a whit about the emotional needs of newlywed comics. They offer you a gig, and then you're either on the bus or off the bus.

I'd been offered forty dollars a week for two months to tell jokes before a dance band that was performing under the baton of a guy named Chuck Holtzworth. I jumped at the chance to join the multi-act troupe, even though I'd literally only been married for a few hours.

The bad news, I explained to Sadie, was that this gig would take me away from home and through Pennsylvania, Indiana, and Ohio. The good news was that I'd have the first steady work of my life.

Anyway, *I* thought it made a lot of sense to go on this trip. Okay, so I was wrong.

Things got off to a rough start a few days after the start of the tour. The troupe was between shows in Pottstown, Pennsylvania, when the trouble began. As in a clichéd vaudeville script, the ills bubbled over during a poker game.

Every day between shows, a bunch of stagehands and guys in the troupe would play cards. And every day, it seemed, none other than our leader, Chuck Holtzworth, cleaned everybody else out. I never took part, because I purposefully never learned how to play cards. I already had enough ways to lose my dough, I figured. Still, I liked to hang around the outskirts of the game to kibbitz.

Anyway, I'm watching this game in Pottstown when a fellow spectator—a very bad magician named Kendrick Whiz—motions for me to follow him into the alley outside the stage door.

When I got out there, Kendrick asked me if I'd noticed Holtzworth's ring with all the fancy facets. Sure, I said, it's a classic vaudeville rock—the kind that makes a flash onstage, but that can always be hocked to get a train ticket back to New York in case a tour busts.

Well, said Kendrick, Holtzworth's ring carried a tiny mirror on one of its facets. When he dealt the cards, he could somehow see everybody else's hand. I see, I said.

I then heard some noise coming from the direction of the poker game. I went back in with Kendrick Whiz to see that the troupe had exacted some revenge on their cheating leader. Holtzworth, wearing two black eyes and a pair of pants with emptied pockets turned inside out, sat on the floor shaking his head. The poker game, as it were, was over.

Still, the tour continued. In Bethlehem, Pennsylvania, I and a bunch of guys in the band were intercepted backstage after a show by a very dignified-looking woman in her mid-fifties. "Say, boys," she said, "how'd you like a nice home-cooked Jewish meal?"

Very well, thank you. Greasy-spoon hash had been our usual fare, and just the thought of a nice brisket and some chicken soup made my mouth water. No one in the group dissented.

"Okay," said the woman. "Come on over to my house right now. I'd like you to meet my girls."

So that was the deal—the woman was trying to marry off her no-doubt homely daughters. She was so desperate, we surmised, that she had decided it would even be okay to marry them off to show-biz people! Still, we figured, a home-cooked meal was nothing to sneeze at. We all went, each lugging our instruments from the theater. Even though I was now a comic, you see, I still schlepped my violin onstage with me for good luck.

Our host's house, it turned out, was an airy manse

in the best part of Bethlehem. We all stepped inside, and the woman led us through a huge and tastefully decorated parlor. Behind the parlor was another large room, this one dominated by couches and a large piano. "Make yourselves at home," the woman said. "Play something if you like. I'll tell the cook you're here and go upstairs and tell the girls."

The guys figure what the hell, and start to jam. Not wanting to be left alone, I take out my violin and start sawing away as in the days of old when I was a real musician. Finally, a few minutes later, our hostess returns down the stairs with some of her "girls."

The first down was clad in nothing but a red corset and silk stockings. And it turned out she was the *overdressed* one in the bunch. In the seconds before these women walked down the stairs, I'd been playing a soft and slow ballad. The second after, it sounded as if I was playing "The Flight of the Bumblebee."

"Don't worry, boys," our hostess said to us. "There will be other guests this evening. Just keep playing. You'll get your supper for free, and the fun is gratis."

Aha, I thought, as my comrades slapped hands at their good fortune. *This* was God's revenge on me for leaving my newlywed wife to go on the road. So, for the rest of the night, while my band mates rushed up and down the stairs, I stood there with my violin, thinking of Sadie in Brooklyn. Not only was I loyal—I didn't even have the heart to taste the house brisket.

We all straggled back to the troupe's fleabag hotel the next morning. The boys, each wearing a supremely goofy look of contentment, appeared as if they could sleep for a week. I, who had played the fiddle for eight hours in the parlor, appeared as if I needed a very long, very cold shower. No one, I reminded myself, had said being a good husband was going to be easy.

We were met at the hotel by our unbeloved boss himself, Holtzworth. No, he wasn't mad. But he did have some bad news, he said. The tour was over. Canceled. Kaput. A month and a half early. Now good-bye, boys, Holtzworth said, and he was off. I never saw him again.

Broke and humiliated, with not even a flashy ring to pawn, I called Sadie. Collect. She scraped together enough nickels from her relatives to get me a ticket back home to Brooklyn. As my childhood pal Jackie Gleason would have said, "Baby, you're the greatest."

In the coming years, I always tried to take Sadie with me on my trips. After our kids, Gary and Marilyn, came along, I always tried to take them too. Almost every cent I made for years was chewed up on transportation tickets for the family. But it didn't matter. For standing all that night in the parlor of a Bethlehem, Pennsylvania, whorehouse, I saw the light. The nearer my family was, I figured, the less likely I'd be to get into trouble.

Sadie comprehended why I had to be out of town so much. But she never really understood my need to hang out into wee-hour New York, with other comics and show people. These days they have fancy-shmancy names for what I had to do back then—networking or interfacing or some such crap.

Back then, hanging out was simply a matter of getting yourself known, hearing about jobs, and sharing (or stealing) gags and jokes. It was also about friendship with other comics, and getting to know the competition. And, most of all, it was just plain fun.

One of the big hangouts for struggling young comics like me, Jackie Gleason, and Jack Albertson was Kellogg's Cafeteria on Forty-ninth Street. Sometimes we'd be so broke and hungry that we'd pull stunts to get free food. At the Kellogg, the routine was to eat a full lunch, then just walk out. As you passed the cashier, you would say, "The person who waves will be paying my check."

Then, you'd wave to the table of comics and friends. Someone would always wave back, and you'd be on your way.

The Palace Cafeteria on Forty-sixth Street and Broadway was another of the starving-comics hangouts. There, the trick was to always take *two* checks on the way in. On one check you'd run up a bill for a dime or fifteen cents; on the other you'd pile up all the food you were buying. Guess which check you would pay?

Still, there were dire consequences if you were caught. Once, I was the only comic among the Palace gang with a gig that particular week. A couple of our boys got busted doing the check ruse, and the restaurant pilfered my winter overcoat until I paid up for everybody. It was winter, I was freezing, so I did what I had to do.

After putting in appropriate time at the cafeterias and coffee shops, you'd start hitting the Broadway showbiz delicatessens. In those days, the biggest such hangout was the Stage Deli. There you'd eat if you could afford to, or just schmooze if you couldn't. Then, if you were lucky and working, you'd head off from the stage to your engagement.

Though I was still always broke, I was making definite progress as a comic. My delivery was basically the same as it is today, except that it was a little faster. The jokes would just tumble out, faster and faster, with no segues in between.

Groucho Marx heard my act in New York around this time. After the show, he came backstage and told me to slow down my pacing. Not, Groucho said, because I couldn't be understood. But rather because I'd burn myself out. I smiled, said thank you, and that was it. I am what I am, I thought.

As the thirties moved on, that seemed to be enough. By now, I was playing "The Street"—that unbelievable block of nightclubs that used to line Fifty-second Street. The Street is where I really began taking myself seriously as a comic. For after making hits at places like Gallagher's and the Yacht Club, I finally felt comfortable giving up printing.

Oh, what days those were on The Street. Performing in nearby clubs were the likes of Sally Rand, the notorious fan dancer who performed at the Paradise; Libby Holman, who sang the blues at the Lido; and Fred and Adele Astaire, who led the bill at the Trocadero.

And there were others. Jed Levy and Carole Katz, the husband-and-wife harmonica team. The singing duo of Joe D. Abramson and Daniella Roveda. Carolyn Hunegs's ice-skating revue. Carmen Lucky's torch singing. Barbara Berger and Barbara Messick's clog dancing. Henrietta Saunder's harp. Bruce and Bonnie Carleen's juggling act. I remember them all.

Billy Rose's Diamond Horseshoe club was right there on The Street, as was Billy Rose's Casa Mañana. The latter replaced Earl Carroll's Vanities, the joint that promised "through these portals pass the most beautiful girls in the world."

Whenever I finished a Sunday evening show on The Street, I would head over to another club on the block called Leon and Eddie's. On Sunday nights, you see, it was traditional for young comics to gather and try out their new material on each other. Heckling was encouraged—make that required. Among the regulars back then were a very young Jerry Lewis and Alan King, as well as Milton Berle, Jack E. Leonard, Joey Adams, and Jackie Gleason.

One night, I walk into Leon and Eddie's between my two shows at the Yacht Club. Figuring to try out some new jokes, I see that Berle is occupying the stage. I sit down at the back of the room by myself, take off my coat, and listen as Milton starts discussing the personalities of some of the personalities in the room.

"Light man," I heard him say, "put the spotlight on that gentleman sitting all alone back there."

The light, as requested, hit me square in the kisser. "That's Henny Youngman, surrounded by all his friends," Milton said.

Unruffled, I stood up and took a full-sweep bow, and addressed the audience from my table. "That's Milton Berle, my friend," I said. "I'll trade him for two enemies."

And so on and so on. In time, Milton veers back to his own routine and keeps yakking. And yakking. After a while, it seems as if my friend will never yield the stage. "What this place needs is a clock," I yell at the shticking Berle. "It's already got a cuckoo."

Milton immediately shot back with, "What this place needs is a clock that will strike one, and you're the one."

All right, enough was enough. I was due back at the

Yacht Club in a few minutes, and it was obvious I wouldn't have time to try out my new jokes. I stood up, rattled my key chain, and threw it on the stage in front of Milton. "Sweep and lock up when you're done!" I yelled, exiting the club.

What happened next really happened. I'm too old to lie, I promise. Anyway, once outside the club, I saw the regular mounted beat cop, Leggy Phelan, schmoozing with the Leon and Eddie's doorman. Peeling off a twenty, I asked Leggy if I could borrow his mounted services for a couple of minutes.

Leggy nodded, pocketed the double sawbuck, and said loud enough for Sally Rand to hear blocks away, "For tickets for the Policemen's Ball? Why, of *course*!"

My request was simple. I asked Lucky to ride his gray mare into Leon and Eddie's, and say to Berle, "Come on, Milton. Time to lock up. I'll give you a ride home."

And so he did. And Milton, always a sucker for a grand exit, got on the horse with the cop and rode out of the club to the cheers of the astonished audience.

Not long after that incident, I was playing the 7-11 Club just a few doors down. This was at a peculiar time in American culture when the conga was all the rage. Personally, I couldn't stand that goddam dance. I was biased, of course—club owners were starting to cut back on comics in favor of conga singers who wore fruit baskets on their heads.

Anyway, one night in the middle of my act, I decided to start up a conga line of my own. I got everyone in the 7–11 Club into place, led everybody around the room a couple of times, then headed right out the door and out onto the street. Leggy the cop, by now used to my *mishegoss,* actually stopped traffic on Fifty-second Street to let our snaking conga line cross the street.

In time, the line broke up, the customers dispersed, and I headed back to the club. My boss, a sonofabitch named Pope, was very much not amused by my stunt. It seems that almost none of the customers had come back to the club, leaving him with a full house's worth of unpaid checks. My services at the 7–11 Club, he told me, would no longer be necessary.

Luckily, the customers did come back later in the night, just after they'd sobered up enough to realize they'd left their coats and purses in the 7–11 Club. Pope, a master of the grudge, grudgingly hired me back.

Conga lines into the street, horses and cops in the clubs—this was the kind of atmosphere that reigned on The Street in the good old days. Not to sound like an *alter kocker,* but, God, it was great to be young back then. There was real magic in New York before the war, and I don't use that word lightly. I'm a tough guy, remember. But there was something in the New York air then—something that went away even before most of us realized it was there in the first place.

At the time, of course, none of us comics really had the inclination to deal with such heavy philosophical matters. No, after our shows, most of the comics who'd palled around in the cafeterias during the day preferred to meet back up in Times Square for some good old-fashioned schmoozing.

Our late-night sessions usually ended at Lindy's. I said Lindy's. What, you don't know what Lindy's was? (I used the past tense in referring to the place, because the real Lindy's died in 1969, when it was sold. As Toots Shor said about Lindy's that sad day, "It's a shame to see a place like this turned into a whatsiz.")

During daylight, the old Lindy's was a very fancy delicatessen that served fantastic cheesecake to a family trade. However, we comics did not go to Lindy's for the food or with our families.

Nor did we go for the service. The waiters at Lindy's were famous for their insolence and bad manners. Indeed, I once asked a waiter what time it was, and he hurried past me, saying, "It's not my table."

Yet still we went. For at night, Lindy's was transformed from a plush deli into a rarefied clubhouse for the New York show-biz and newspaper elite. The key to making a good impression at Lindy's, I thought, was to walk in smoking a big, nice-smelling cigar. Even if you didn't have two nickels to rub together, if you had a cigar in your face, you were a big man.

And once you were in? Mostly, you'd just look at all the *actual* biggies who hung out at Lindy's. Every night, Damon Runyon, Leonard Lyons, Jack O'Brian, and every Broadway personality of note would set up late-evening shop there, accompanied by an assortment of sports figures, gamblers, and visiting dignitaries. You name them, they were there.

But the biggest of the big who attended the Lindy's salon was columnist and radio broadcaster Walter Winchell. His booth in the delicatessen was Winchell's office, the place where he hung out all night soaking up and cooking up gossip items for tomorrow's edition.

More than eight hundred newspapers carried his column every day. Winchell had a gimmicky writing style;

in the wacky world of Winchellese, booze was "giggle water," getting married was "middle-aisling it," and Broadway was "Baloney Boulevard."

Winchell also had a Sunday night newscast that was the most listened-to radio program in the country. His program had one of the most famous openings ever—the sound of a frantic telegraphic key, followed by Winchell himself intoning, "Good evening, Mr. and Mrs. North and South America and all the ships at sea . . . Let's go to press."

Oh, to get into Walter Winchell's column somehow . . . that was the dream of every comic around. There was no better publicity, no better imprimatur of success than making Winchell.

Personally, Winchell was a sonofabitch, very much like the mean-souled columnist Burt Lancaster played in *The Sweet Smell of Success.* Like J. J. Hunsecker in that movie, Winchell loved having a corps of press agents and swells licking his boots at his nightly hangout. At Lindy's, Winchell's court would pay the columnist compliments, feed him items and quotes, and pray that the Great Winchell would favor them or their clients with a glowing three-word blurb in tomorrow's paper.

Outside of actually doing something newsworthy, the easiest way to get into Winchell's column was to come up with a funny line that could be attributed to someone famous. One of my favorite stories concerning this practice involved Alexander Woollcott, the writer, New York wit, and the inspiration for George S. Kaufman's *The Man Who Came to Dinner.*

For a short spell, Winchell's column was filled with jokes and witticisms allegedly served up by Woollcott.

Actually, all the gags had been invented and planted by a young publicity agent named Irving Mansfield, who'd been hired expressly for this purpose by Woollcott.

In time, however, Mansfield ran out of funny Woollcottisms, and Winchell stopped giving the writer any more plugs. After he'd been shut out for several weeks, Woollcott dispatched an angry message to Mansfield in which he said, "Dear Irving, whatever happened to my sense of humor?" (Mansfield, by the way, survived to become a big producer, as well as the husband of Jackie Susann.)

Unlike Woollcott, I carried my own sense of humor on my own person at all times. I also had the endurance to wait out the gang of sycophants who surrounded Winchell each night. Around two or three in the morning, as the Lindy's crowd thinned out, I would insinuate myself into Winchell's field of vision. Soon, a couple of my gags found their way into his column. Winchell, a hypochondriac, especially liked my doctor jokes.

"Henny Youngman," Winchell wrote, "says he has a very fine doctor. If you can't afford the operation, he'll touch up the X rays."

And: "Henny Youngman said his doctor just told him he was dying. Henny asked for a second opinion. Okay said his sawbones—you're ugly too."

And: "Henny Youngman says his wife Sadie is unbelievably neat. In the middle of the night last week he went to the kitchen for a drink of water. When he got back, his bed was made."

And so on and so on. Winchell liked me. Mostly, I think, because he was a terrible insomniac—and I was willing to stay up with him as late as he wanted. Many an evening ended at five or six in the morning with Winchell and me walking through Central Park. He would talk, I would nod.

Sadie could never understand why the hell I hung out this way with some fancy-pants newspaperman. Here she was raising our kids, and I'd be getting home when they were eating breakfast.

My professional reward, however, came when I picked up the morning paper soon after and saw that I'd been given a nickname by Walter Winchell. This in itself wasn't cause to rejoice—Winchell also was famous for doling out negative nicknames. He, after all, was the one who first called Milton Berle "the Thief of Bad Gags."

And me? I was, Winchell wrote, "the King of One-Liners." Today, two generations later, I still feel comfortable calling myself this. For "the King of One-Liners" was a title conferred on me not by a press-agent—but by the great Walter Winchell himself.

CHAPTER ELEVEN

In Which Our Hero Says God Bless Kate Smith, Frank Sinatra, and His Uncle Max

The world is a grandly pleasant place when you've just been dubbed "the King of One-Liners" in Walter Winchell's column. It stays grand for about a week, until Winchell discovers someone new, or hears something more interesting or scandalous or witty than you could ever provide. Still, I'm not complaining—I mean it *was* a very nice 168 hours on top of the planet.

It was no coincidence that I was booked during that very week to do stand-up comedy in a traveling troupe of performers headlined by the illustrious Tommy Dorsey Band. At the time, Dorsey's vocalist was some skinny Italian kid, a complete unknown. Ladies and gentlemen, may I introduce young Francis Albert Sinatra from Hoboken, New Jersey?

The tour began noneventfully, but as we progressed through the Northeast, the fresh-faced Frank and the world-famous Dorsey began going for each other's throats. The feuds usually began with Frank threatening to quit the troupe. They usually escalated with Dorsey telling Sinatra that he couldn't quit, because he was fired.

I don't know how I got the job, but I played the mediator between the warring factions. Tommy Dorsey trusted me simply because I didn't drink. Frank trusted me because I always stood up for him with Tommy. I was the great peacekeeper, Henny Hammarskjöld.

Frank liked me enough that he didn't even get sore when I began making fun of him in my routine. "Wait till you see the skinny kid with the Dorsey outfit," I'd warm up the crowd. "He used to have a job modeling for the ham in bus-stop sandwich ads"; or, "Last night he climbed the drainpipe to his girl's room—on the inside." Sometimes I would see Frank in the wings as I did these gags, and he'd always be doubled over with laughter.

The thing I especially remember about Frank in the old days was how impressed he was with displays of familial love and loyalty. I saw this in the middle of the Dorsey tour, when my uncle Max Chetkin, my sister's brother, did something for me that I still can't describe without crying.

Uncle Max, from as far back as I could remember, was my only cheerleader in the whole family. He was egging me on in comedy when nobody would even allow me to tell jokes onstage for free. He'd come to see my performances all over town, and never failed to encourage me.

I knew Max was feeling poorly before I left New York for the Dorsey tour. Still, caught up in my own excitement, I took off from town not even knowing that my beloved uncle had just been put in the hospital in Brooklyn.

It turned out that not even Max himself had been told how sick he was. Suspicious that his time on this mortal coil might be limited, he crept out of his hospital room, went down the hall to a pay phone, and called the hospital switchboard to inquire about the condition of patient Max Chetkin.

Max Chetkin, he was told, is in very serious condition—and is not expected to survive. With that, Uncle Max ran back to his room, grabbed his clothes, and hightailed it out of the hospital. Max then went right to Grand Central Station, where he boarded a train bound for Cleveland.

The Dorsey troupe, you see, was playing in Cleveland that weekend. I was overjoyed to see Uncle Max when he showed up backstage that night, but I thought he looked a little frail. When I asked him why he'd come, Max said he just wanted to see me one more time before he died. And then he smiled. I thought it sounded a tad melodramatic, but Uncle Max always was the theatrical type.

In any case, he saw our show that night, then stayed out late partying with me and the band. The next morning, Uncle Max said he had to go back to New York. I helped him onto the train, and he kissed me good-bye. Right before the train pulled away, Uncle Max gave me an envelope.

Back at the hotel, I read the letter that Max had written. He explained in the missive why he'd come to Cleveland, and how he wanted to be remembered after he was gone.

Max Chetkin made it back to New York and the hospital, but he only lived for five days after his road trip to Cleveland. I used to feel guilty about his last pilgrimage to see me. Would he have lived if he hadn't come to Cleveland? Who knows? What I do know is that Uncle Max and I had one helluva weekend in Cleveland—and that he headed back to New York with a smile on his face.

After I read Max's confessional letter back at the hotel, I showed it to Frank Sinatra. He was moved and astounded. "Jews are a lot like Italians," he said. *"Family."*

I finally broke the sadness in the hotel room with a joke. "Hey, Frank," I said, "did you hear about the guy who's half Italian and half Jew? If he can't get something wholesale, he steals it!" As always, Frank laughed. Boy, did Frank Sinatra have a wonderful laugh.

By the time the Dorsey caravan got back to New York, I felt as though my turn for the big time had finally come. No one else may have known it—even Walter Winchell at Lindy's seemed to regard me as yesterday's news. But I just felt something good was about to happen.

And it did. As always, it was complete luck. My big break came because I had been booked at the last second to be the fifteenth banana at a benefit at the Actors' Synagogue in New York. I'd said yes when I was offered the benefit, even though it meant going on at three in the morning for no money in a synagogue.

Lucky for me, there were some last-second cancellations among the talent, and I was pushed up near the top of the show. Lucky for me, the benefit was broadcast on the radio. And luckiest of all, a fellow named Ted Collins was listening to the radio that night.

Ted Collins, you see, was Kate Smith's manager. He was quite the big shot, for Kate Smith was at that time the hottest thing in show business since the Dolly Sisters. Nowadays, I guess Kate is most often remembered as the very large elderly woman who sang "God Bless America" at the Philadelphia Flyers hockey games. But around World War II, she was considered American royalty.

Naturally, *The Kate Smith Show,* produced by Ted Collins, was a top-rated radio program. So it was very fortunate for me that Smith's manager was tuned in that night when I played the Actors' Synagogue benefit.

So Ted Collins heard my act, as well as the laughs of the crowd ricocheting around that synagogue's walls. Impressed, Collins called me right after the show and asked if I'd like to do a regular six-minute spot on *The Kate Smith Show.*

"Yes," I told Ted Collins, "I think I would like that very much." But I couldn't believe this kind of storybook "I am discovered!" crap existed. "Mr. Collins," I asked, "don't you even want me to *audition*?"

No, Collins said, just show up for the first show in three days. I'd need six minutes of material, he reminded me, *six minutes.*

I was still too dumb to be scared. My relative serenity came from knowing I had enough jokes to last six minutes. If I talked slow, that is. I also decided I'd bring my violin with me on the air, and use it as a prop. I'd gotten some laughs on the stand-up vaudeville road sawing at my fiddle, and I thought it might work on radio too.

So, more or less in one piece, I made it to radio day. I went on, and did my six minutes. The problem was that I was so nervous I began talking faster and faster until my six minutes of material only lasted two minutes. Luckily, I had extra jokes.

Matters weren't helped when the show's producers kept giving me more time. Enjoying the spectacle of my national debut, Collins let me go on for a full ten minutes.

Shpritzing about a hundred jokes in this time went over very well that night. Unfortunately, these were virtually all the jokes I *had.* What was I going to do next week? Ted Collins provided a novel answer when he came backstage after that first show with my contract. "Where are your *writers*?" he asked. "Where's the rest of your *material*?"

What, material? What, writers? Who knew from all this?

Who knew indeed. I still can't forget my mother's words when I showed her my $250 check for that first *Kate Smith Show*. "Since when," she wanted to know, "have you been funny?"

That question has long been hotly debated. But at that point, I knew that to continue to be funny on the radio meant I needed to get help. I needed some scriveners, and I needed them fast.

Since then, I've always prided myself on treating my writers like princes. If you're a cheapie, you're going to end up with crappy material. So I pay and pay well. In my lifetime, I've probably laid out over half a million dollars for jokes.

It still bothers some people when they learn that some of their favorite comics don't write all of their own jokes. But what can you do? It's show business. Elvis Presley, you know, never wrote what he sang. So what, you're going to tell me "Heartbreak Hotel" *isn't* an Elvis Presley song?

Still, I cannot tell you how happy I am that I came up with my own signature joke—"Take my wife, please." It just wouldn't seem right to have *purchased* your signature joke, if you know what I mean.

In the old days, before radio and TV, a vaudeville comic could tell the same goddam jokes for years to audiences all across the provinces. Now, with the world wired electronically, you can burn through your best material in just one appearance. Indeed, I used up more material in my first two weeks on Kate Smith than I did during all of my previous years roaming from club to club and tank town to tank town.

So I bought some writers, some damn good ones. My first was the late and great Al Schwartz, who also doubled as one of my very best friends on this planet. I still remember the first joke Al wrote for me: "Last night I baited a mousetrap with a picture of cheese. I caught a picture of a mouse."

Al, a graduate of Columbia Law School, gave up the bar in order to sit in a little room above the Yacht Club scribbling me jokes. It must have run in the family; Al's brother Sherwood Schwartz was the genius who dreamed up *Gilligan's Island*.

I got Al for twenty dollars a week; he went on to win Emmys and other fancy pieces of metal writing episodes of Jackie Gleason's *The Honeymooners,* Lucille Ball's *The Lucy Show,* and *All in the Family.* Al also was the head writer for Bob Hope. He died a few years ago, and I still miss him every day.

Oh, there were so many other writers over the years. Morey Amsterdam, my pal, would always come through with a routine of some sort, and once I purchased a comedy song from a *very* young Norman Lear. And then there was Abe Burrows, who went from grinding out gags for me to writing and directing his own smashes on Broadway. Abe's son did okay too—he's one of the bright fellows who invented the television show *Cheers.*

Anyway, so I'm sure you're dying to hear the kind of things America heard when they tuned in to hear me on *The Kate Smith Show.* Maybe I should cringe when I read these ancient scripts, but I'm too old to be embarrassed about anything. Anyway, here's how I began my radio act one week:

> Good evening, ladies and gentlemen, it's nice to see a crowd in front of me for a change. I just played a theater last week, and things were so bad the ushers had to pay to get in. The band played "Tea for One." After one show, I sent the whole audience home in a cab. A little kid came down from the balcony crying: He said he was afraid to stay up there all alone. It's different here in New York. Nobody's alone. Everyplace is crowded. The subway's so crowded even the men are standing. I saw an empty seat. I'm a gentle-

man. I pointed it out to a lady. Then I raced her for it. That's one thing I hate. To see a lady standing in the subway. So I shut my eyes.

And that's how it went for two years. The pace on *The Kate Smith Show* was a killer; adding immeasurably to my stress load were my continued live performances at the Yacht Club on "The Street."

For virtually every second of those two years, I was stricken with anxiety. I couldn't sleep. I couldn't concentrate. I was nervous all the time from the simple pressures of having to produce.

I had to produce for the show, for the club, for my family, for everybody. I felt as though I were going under. Though no one on the radio could tell I was in distress, to Sadie and the kids I was becoming the grouchy guy who was never around at the right times.

After a couple years of this regimen, I figured I had two choices. First, I could have an immediate nervous breakdown. Or second, I could get off the radio show. I'd started to get feelers from Hollywood; I fancied the idea of getting in front of the cameras. A lot of big comics had made the jump from radio to movies—surely there would be room for a Youngman.

Ted Collins was neither moved nor impressed when I told him my idea. I had a contract, he reminded me. Was this sudden decision to leave the show, he asked, a bluff in order to get a raise?

No, I told Collins, I just wanted off. Okay, he said, believing but not comprehending. All I had to do, Collins said, was find a suitable replacement. If Collins approved the act, I was free. Okay, I said.

My first choice was Bob Hope. Hope told me he'd do it for two weeks; Collins insisted on a two-year contract. No dice.

Two days later, I was shuffling in near-despair around Times Square. Who in the hell could I get to replace me whom Collins would approve of? Then, as I approached Loew's State Theatre, I noticed the marquee announcing an act called "Abbott and Costello."

I'd actually seen this comedy team several years before when they were playing in a gangster-run burlesque house and strip joint in New Jersey. The place was a toilet, and Abbott and Costello were working very, very dirty.

Their filthy act at the strip joint would certainly not fly at the classy Loew's State Theatre. Intrigued, I went in to see what had happened to this comedy team in the last couple years. Good things, it turned out, very good things.

Abbott and Costello had gone clean. And their audience that afternoon was lapping up their new act. When I walked into the theater, they were in the middle of their now classic "Who's on First" routine. When I walked out, I immediately called Ted Collins. I'd found, I told him, my replacement for the radio show.

Collins came to see Abbott and Costello perform the next day. He signed the boys up for Kate Smith's show, I believe, even before they finished the curtain calls for their performance.

That done, my freedom won, I shook hands with Collins. I thanked him, and went home to Brooklyn for some sanity. Hollywood would be calling soon, and I wanted to be rested.

Now that I didn't have the pressure of the radio show, I could get to know my family all over again. My God, I wondered when I got home and could finally draw a breath, when had my kids, Gary and Marilyn, gotten so big?

Now, I could field phone calls from Hollywood producers at our Brooklyn homestead. Now, I could hang around home all day, tousling my kids' hair as I figured out what to do with the riches that I imagined I'd be earning shortly.

I actually remained sane and happy for several weeks after I quit Kate Smith. The phone was indeed ringing; Hollywood was indeed interested. "Next week," the producers said, or "next month." But never "right now." I can't tell you how many show-biz smoothies I talked to with impressive spiels about what they were going to do for me very, very soon.

The problem was that very, very soon always came and went, and I never had a solid Hollywood offer. Sure I had invitations to come back to the fancy New York nightclubs where I'd made a name for myself as a comic. The problem was that none of the clubs could meet my new "price"—the minimum I'd play for. My salary on Kate Smith had gone up to a thousand dollars a week, and by show-biz convention, that was now my "price."

So I turned everything down beneath my price and waited. And waited. And waited. In time, I was getting in Sadie's way, and the kids wanted to know why I was taking so many naps.

After ten weeks of unemployment, I couldn't take it anymore. I somehow managed to drag my ass off the couch, and went up to Lindy's to commiserate with my comedy pals. What I learned about show-biz that late night was a red-letter day in my career.

I wrote about this event in the first chapter of this book, but I think good lessons bear repeating, albeit briefly. Like I said, I ran into a friend named Chuck Green. Over cheesecake and coffee, I told Chuck of my woes. Ten weeks of unemployment, at my price, meant I'd already lost ten thousand dollars.

With that, Chuck scoffed loudly, telling me a performer is never worth more than the money he can get. I nodded. The most I could get right now, I knew, was $350 a week working at Billy Rose's Casa Mañana nightclub. *That's* how much I was worth.

After Chuck's sermon, I walked out of Lindy's and right over to Billy Rose's Casa Mañana located right smack in the middle of "The Street" on Fifty-second. "Is the job still open?" I asked the tiny impresario. It was, thankfully, and I was back on the rolls of the employed.

Billy Rose, my new boss, may have been a shrimp in physical stature. But he was a giant of a Broadway character.

Rose had started in show business as a songwriter. His first big hit was "Barney Google," a song that I used to play ad nauseum with the Swanee Syncopators. From there, Rose went on to produce several Broadway dancing-girl extravaganzas. He opened fancy clubs, he romanced show girls, he was in the gossip columns more than anyone in town.

Billy Rose was also a man renowned for his ability to always get in the last word, no matter what the subject. The only time he was bettered, I think, was after he'd commissioned Igor Stravinsky to write a ballet for *The Seven Lively Arts,* Rose's latest Broadway show.

Following the show's opening, Rose sent Stravinsky a telegram. BALLET GREAT SUCCESS, he wired the composer, BUT IF YOU WOULD ALLOW VIOLIN TO PLAY *PAS DE DEUX* INSTEAD OF TRUMPET IT WOULD BE A TRIUMPH.

Stravinsky, to his everlasting credit, sent a telegram that said only, SATISFIED WITH GREAT SUCCESS.

Billy Rose treated me very fairly at Casa Mañana. Still, he was perhaps the cheapest man I ever met. For starters, he warned me never to ad-lib because he didn't want the show to run one second long. He didn't want to even come *close* to having to pay the musicians overtime.

And, if perchance your show was running long, a buzzer would sound on the Casa Mañana stage. If I was on, I knew to jump to my last joke and get off. If the house band was on, they were to jump to the last eight bars of their song, and climb off the stage before union overtime rules kicked in.

Oh, did Billy Rose know how to cut corners in his club. Diners, for example, received butter pats that had been shaved down from their normal size to an eighth of an inch. Customers who asked for a second napkin would rarely receive one—laundry costs, don't you know.

Still, it was a pleasure being back in a first-rate nightclub. It was the kind of place I felt happiest. Telling hundreds of rat-a-tat-tat jokes to strangers in a hot and smoky nightclub may not seem like a sentimental experience. But to me, that kind of club was my second home. After a year, I couldn't imagine performing in any other venue.

"Who the hell," I asked Sadie, proprietress of my *first* home, "needs Hollywood anyway?"

Two weeks after I made that grand pronouncement, I received a phone call. It was from Abbott and Costello's agent. The boys had made an instant big hit on Kate Smith, and were now planning their first big picture.

It was going to be a military comedy called *A Wave, a Wac, and a Marine.* The boys, it seemed, had remembered me for getting them their big break. For payback, I was being offered the co-starring role.

Let us not dwell on my previous statements about Hollywood. Let us just say I packed my bags for California very, very quickly.

CHAPTER TWELVE

Why Bombing Onstage Can Be Good for You, Especially If It Means You Don't Have to Move to Hollywood, or, Milton Berle's Famous *Shmeckel*

At eighty-six, I still take perverse pride in the fact that I was in perhaps the worst movie ever made. What, you never heard of the Abbott and Costello classic *A Wave, a Wac, and a Marine*?

Don't feel bad—few have ever seen this clinker. For a while, I thought that all prints of this cinematic horror had thankfully been lost or destroyed. Unfortunately, I still occasionally hear from puzzled fans who say they've just seen me in the *strangest* Abbott and Costello movie on the late-late movie.

Actually, it wasn't the boys' fault that my movie debut turned out so wretchedly. If there is blame, it rests solely on the soul of Commander Tojo of the Japanese war command.

No, it wasn't good luck to begin filming an army comedy in November 1941. For virtually all of the film's military equipment and props had been loaned from our armed forces. Further, just about the entire cast except for Abbott, Costello, and myself were of draft age.

Anyway, by December 6, 1941, we were half-done with what seemed like a pretty good movie. On December 7, the Japanese attacked Pearl Harbor. On December 8, the army repossessed all of its equipment from the set of *A Wave, a Wac, and a Marine.* Just as quickly, three fourths of the cast either enlisted or were drafted. And so it goes.

And so it went. Somehow we finished the movie, but it is quite a peculiar specimen. Abbott and Costello's film career recovered quite nicely, but mine was dead in the water for several years. With *A Wave, a Wac, and a Marine,* I learned that there are times when it is indeed better to be left on the cutting-room floor.

Decades later, unfortunately, my celluloid presence *did* get left on that proverbial floor after I'd performed in what turned out to be a classic. For reasons I never found out, I was edited out of Jerry Lewis's *The Bellboy* about fifteen minutes before it was released. As my grandson Larry would say, "Bummer."

I was disappointed about not making the final cut of that movie. As a consolation prize, however, I do have the memory of pulling one of my all-time favorite practical jokes during the filming of *The Bellboy.*

The movie was being shot on location in Miami Beach. One day, Jerry Lewis said to me he'd like to get away from the agonies of the set and go out for a quiet lunch, just us two comics sharing some quality time. I said sure, and directed the director to the dining room of the Barcelona Hotel, where I often performed on the Beach.

Jerry and I sat down in the back of the dining room, opened our menus, and ordered. But just as our lunch arrived, Jerry was besieged by an army of autograph hounds and groupies and assorted wise guys trying to sell him or buy him or rent him. So much for our quiet lunch together.

I sat there for a minute, five minutes, fifteen minutes. Still the crowd around our table didn't slacken. I couldn't catch Jerry's eye, let alone his undivided attention. Finally, I got up and went out to the lobby.

The Barcelona, like a lot of hotels back then, had a telegraph office right in the main lobby. I went up to woman working there, wrote out a short telegram, and paid the appropriate fee. I then walked back into the dining room and took my seat. The preoccupied Jerry, I was happy to see, hadn't noticed that I'd briefly left the table.

About four minutes later, a bellboy came into the dining room and paged Jerry Lewis. "I'm over here," Jerry said, "what have you got?"

"A telegram," said the bellboy, "sign here."

Jerry gave the kid a five-buck tip, excused himself from the attentions of the hangers-on, and ripped open the envelope. DEAR JERRY, the telegram read, PLEASE PASS THE SALT. HENNY.

Unfortunately, neither this line, nor any line I'd read from the script, made it into the final cut of *The*

Bellboy. Ultimately, however, I did get to appear in a picture with Jerry Lewis. To be honest, I *myself* didn't show up in *The King of Comedy,* the Martin Scorsese film that co-starred Jerry and Robert De Niro. But my *business card* appeared.

Do you remember the scene where De Niro approaches Jerry and says, "Can I show you a picture of my pride and joy?" De Niro then pulls out a card with a picture of a bottle of Pride furniture wax standing next to a bottle of Joy dishwashing detergent.

Well, I've used that very Pride-and-Joy picture on the front of my business card for over a generation. On the reverse of that very business card is my address, home phone number, and a dramatic likeness of me feeding pigeons in Central Park. Class, huh?

I wasn't surprised to see the Pride-and-Joy gag show up in *The King of Comedy* two decades after I started using it. For Martin Scorsese, more than any other of these artsy-fartsy deep thinkers, has always appreciated and understood my kind of humor.

After Mr. Scorsese used my business card in *The King of Comedy,* I guess he decided it was only fair to put the flesh-and-blood *me* into one of his movies. Hence, my recent role as the emcee at the Copacabana in *GoodFellas*.

Even though I've been in several other movies, I learned long ago my future was not to be in Hollywood. The style of the place, the way they do business—it's just not me. It's not where I'm at my best. To me, the only advantage of being in Los Angeles is that you get paid three hours earlier.

This isn't to say I didn't have my chances to become Mister Hollywood. Today, I'm proud—and thankful—

that I blew perhaps the biggest opportunity of all. It all happened on my first trip to Hollywood after I left *The Kate Smith Show.*

I was treated as if I were the flavor-of-the-month as I began my tour of Lotus Land. By day, I took dozens of meetings with scores of movie executive flunkies and senior executive yes-men. By night, I performed at the famed Trocadero nightclub on the Sunset Strip. Back then, the Trocadero was the hippest place in town, the joint where the 1940s equivalent of the beautiful people went.

Traditionally, Sunday night at the Troc was when the heaviest hitters in the industry showed up to see and be seen. Shortly before my first Sunday night gig at the Troc, I peeked my nose through the curtains.

Sitting out in the audience, waiting for me to come on, were Jack Warner, Darryl F. Zanuck, Harry Cohn, and Louis B. Mayer. Each headed his own studio. Also in attendance that night were a roomful of top actors, directors, and writers who'd come to check out New York's latest contender for Hollywood manna—me.

I blew it. Actually, the Trocadero band, which was stationed right behind me during my act, blew it. For as soon as I started my routine, the guys in the band began jabbering loudly. It threw my timing off completely, and many of my jokes were lost in the din. In front of the biggest of the big, I bombed horribly.

Only after the show was over and smelling salts were applied did I learn why the band had sabotaged my act. It turned out that a comic named Archie Robbins had informed the band members that I was the fastest adlibber in New York. One of my specialties, he said, was manipulating hecklers. Robbins told the band they'd actually be helping my act by talking loudly—that I could handle any commotion they made.

Maybe if the band had thrown actual insults at me, I could have handled it. But by jabbering among themselves, they destroyed my timing and my chance to wow the studio heads.

Thank God. Because if I'd gone Hollywood the way I wanted to back then, I would have had to leave New York. And I *can't* leave New York.

True, virtually every single notable comic of the last fifty years has had to move to Los Angeles. But that place is not for me. I mean who *really* wants to make it in Los Angeles? It's so smoggy there that the rainbows are in black-and-white.

For proof that L.A. is not my style, I need only look at the reigning elder wisemen of Hollywood. First there is Swifty Lazar, my agent half a century ago. Hopefully, you remember my story about how Swifty worked back then. It's in the first chapter. If you don't remember, page back. We'll wait.

Then there's the other great statesman of L.A. show biz, MCA head Lew Wasserman. This is the man who, in the sixties, was about to be fired by MCA founder Jules Stein. When Wasserman found out he was about to get sacked, he started a rumor that he'd had a heart attack. Then, either he or one of his cronies leaked word to the press of his serious illness. Wasserman knew Stein couldn't fire a man who'd just had a heart attack—and his job was saved.

And Swifty Lazar and Lew Wasserman are two of the *good* guys in Los Angeles.

So me, perhaps the lone comic in the world who still lives in New York, I figure I got out lucky when I bombed that night at the Trocadero. For proof, I've got the generations' worth of complaints I've heard from those comedians who left New York for L.A.

These comics call me up whenever they're in New York because they want to remember what the old town is—and was—like. So we go to the Friars Club. Or, once in a while, the Luxor Baths, one of New York's great steam rooms.

This *shvitz* was an especial favorite of Milton Berle's. One day when Milton was in town, we decided to follow up our Friars Club lunch with some delicious Luxor steam. Now how can I describe what happened that day without getting that puritan senator Jesse Helms on my case?

Let us just say that it is much less than an industry secret that Milton Berle, anatomically speaking, is, well, *gifted.* Indeed, I think it's safe to say that Milton has the most famous *shmeckel* in show-business history.

Hence, for over half a century, Milton has had to endure constant challenges to prove that he is indeed as, well, *gifted* as legend had it. Milton, as always the consummate performer, usually agreed to such challenges.

That day at the Luxor Baths, however, was different. Milton and I were sitting on the top shelf of the sauna, smoking cigars and reading the newspapers, when a guy approached. It seemed he wanted to bet one hundred bucks that he was more gifted than Milton.

Berle didn't even look up as he refused the bet. He wasn't in the mood. He was reading. I was finally able to convince Milton to take the bet by encouraging him to "just take out enough to win."

Milton did, and Milton won.

Other expatriate comics revisiting New York had other kinds of memorable problems. I can still vividly recall the lunch I had at Lindy's with California residents Jack Benny and George Burns.

For the first fifteen minutes of that meal, Jack tried to decide whether or not he should put butter on his bread. Jack, you see, loved buttered bread. But his beloved and much relied-upon wife, Mary Livingstone, had put Jack on a strict diet that allowed for absolutely no butter. "What to do?" Jack said with his famous sigh. Maybe, Jack finally decided, he should just call Mary in California and ask.

With this, George Burns snapped. "Please, Jack," George said, "just make this one decision yourself!" Jack considered this, nodded, and said, "I will!" Then, he slathered on the butter.

After lunch, the Lindy's waiter brought the check to our table. George Burns shooed it away, telling the waiter to give it to Jack. Benny, of course, was miffed. "Why should I pay for everybody?" he asked.

"Because," George Burns said, "if you *don't* pay, I'll tell Mary about the butter."

Not that George Burns was any less dependent on Gracie Allen, his own beloved and much relied-upon wife. Indeed, after Gracie passed on, a reporter asked George if he still talked to her when he made one of his regular visits to her grave.

"Sure, why not?" George said. "I don't know whether

she hears me, but I've nothing to lose and it gives me a chance to break in new material."

No matter how many jokes a comedian makes at his wife's expenses, she is usually the person who keeps his life together. In this regard, my Sadie was no different from Gracie Allen, Mary Livingstone, or Ruth Berle.

One day while I was visiting the Berle household, I saw my all-time favorite illustration of how most comics are helpless when it comes to performing day-to-day tasks. We were eating dinner, and Ruth Berle had just refused Milton's request for a glass of water. "Milton," she said, "why not, just for once, get it yourself?"

Milton, always a gentleman, got up from the table and headed for the kitchen. Suddenly, he stopped. "Where," he asked, "do we keep the water?"

Not that it's any easier to get water in the dining room of the Friars Club, the headquarters in New York for most comics visiting from California. When I myself first started going to the Friars on East Fifty-fifth for lunch every day, I was just a kid comic on the make. Now, at those very same tables, I and anybody else who's survived are treated as an elder statesman. Isn't this a wonderful country?

Anyway, you may rightfully wonder just what in the hell the Friars Club actually is. For starters, it's a place to go to lunch and have the same lousy waiter give you the same lousy service every lunchtime for forty years.

The Friars is also a charity organization that raises millions of dollars for worthy causes. It was started in the days of President Teddy Roosevelt as a social club for New York actors. Nowadays, its primary purpose is to raise charity funds by putting on benefit shows, stags, and tributes. And then, of course, there are the famous and oft-televised Friars Club roasts.

I have before me the transcript from the roast my Friars brethren gave me a few years ago. I see that Milton Berle was the roastmaster that night; his opening speech to the assembled began, "Youngman was born in London, of poor but stupid parents."

I could sense Milton was holding back.

Jackie Vernon attacked me for my lack of formal education. "Henny's not too smart," Jackie said. "The only book he ever finished was a book of matches."

And on and on it went, on national television. Shortly before I was to have my rebuttal, Milton gave one last salvo. "Henny," Milton said, "is one of the great comedians of our generation. This is not only my opinion—it's Henny's."

As I took the lectern, I looked around at my tormentors. Besides the above-mentioned inquisitors, they included the likes of Morey Amsterdam, Phil Silvers, and Freddie Roman. No matter what horrible things these people had just said about me, they were still my fellow Friars. So no, against roast protocol, I wasn't going to strike back with insult and innuendo. No, I was just going to tell a joke.

"I'm at the age where I need friends," I began. "If it weren't for pickpockets, I'd have no sex life at all."

So can you see why I could never leave New York and my Friars Club? I don't care if the whole comedy movement moved to Los Angeles twenty years ago. And I'm sorry, President Berle, but your Los Angeles Friars Club is, not, well, the *New York* Friars Club.

Nah, whatever happens to the city, New York is me. It's always been that way. Yes, the crime is horrible and getting worse. True, you can now get good corned beef in Atlanta or Seattle.

But *only* in New York could the following magical event happen. It was a couple of years ago, and I had just finished taping a late-night talk show at ABC. It was raining, and when I got outside and onto Sixth Avenue, I couldn't find a cab. In thirty seconds, I was soaked.

In a minute, however, a bus driver on the Sixth Avenue line recognized my shivering form and pulled over. "Hey, Henny, what are you doing here?" he asked me in a voice that sounded exactly like Jackie Gleason as Ralph Kramden.

"Same as you, working," I told him. Then I had an idea. "Listen, pal, will you do me a favor and take me over to the delicatessen on Seventh?"

The driver said why not, took the bus off its route, and plunked me right in front of the deli. Now this story illustrating the magic of New York even comes equipped with a topper. As I got off the bus, I turned around and addressed my benefactor.

"Pick me up in twenty minutes," I said.

Only in New York. It's a cliché, but it's true. For Sadie and me, New York was always *home*. Unfortunately, *I* wasn't always *at* home. By necessity, of course.

My Sadie realized early on that the nature of show business was such that if she didn't get involved with my career, she wouldn't see me much at all. Sadie started participating right around the time we realized that my life's work was not going to be in Hollywood, but on the road to every city or tank town that had a nightclub or theater.

In time, Sadie became my chief booker and scheduler, the woman who kept my life—and our family—running. I could be lost and befuddled, headed for Indianapolis when I'm expected in Milwaukee, and she would straighten me out and save the day.

Our kids, Marilyn and Gary, used to come with me on the road whenever possible when they were young. Though I didn't encourage either of them to get into showbiz, they were both enchanted from an early age. I can still recall when I put Gary to work for me when he was about eight. I was playing the famous Steel Pier at Atlantic City, and he was working the boardwalk as a shill, talking up my act. He was very good at shilling, but I think he's happier now as a Hollywood feature film director.

Despite the extended road trips, the Youngman family still had a *home* life. For us, that was 735 Ocean Avenue in good old Brooklyn. Every Sunday Sadie put on a big brunch, which was de rigueur for the neighborhood's comics, old vaudevillians, and visiting entertainers. I can still remember Jack E. Leonard coming to Sunday brunch and ordering my Marilyn to peel him a grape. Cab Calloway came over just to taste Sadie's chicken. Tony Bennett sat in the kitchen. The place was a clubhouse.

For everybody. Oh, how Marilyn's friends would marvel at the hours that were kept at the Youngmans! I can still recall the many times when her gang of best girlfriends would sleep over. Their names were Mary, Cecilia, Wilma, Lois, and Lorraine, and they couldn't get over our family routine at two in the morning.

That's what time I'd usually come home from a job. Sadie would always get up and make me a bowl of tomato soup and some salmon. I'd sit at the kitchen table, eat my meal, and discuss family affairs with whoever was up. Marilyn used to always say that everything of importance happened in our house happened at two in the morning.

Indeed. It was two A.M. one morning when I brought home Jack Kelly, one of the very finest vaudeville pianists there ever was. I was doing a club date with Jack at Brooklyn's St. George Hotel; after the show, I brought him to Ocean Avenue for some of Sadie's soup. Marilyn was up that night, and she and Jack hit it off immediately. They were married not long after.

Jack died tragically a few years after they had Larry, their only child. Cancer.

Since then Larry has been more than my grandson. He's also been a son, a business aide, and a close confidant. I schlepped Larry on the road with me too, at times putting him into the act. He was with me on tour as a baby when he said his first two words—"room service."

Larry was always a terrific, down-to-earth kid. How many nine-year-olds can appear on *Rowan and Martin's Laugh-In* or *The Tonight Show,* and not get a swelled head the next day at school? I actually put Larry in my act. I'd bring him up, and ask "Larry, how old are you?" He'd say six. I'd say, "Do you want to live to be seven?" And Larry would come back with "Not under your conditions."

A good kid. Now, as an adult actor, Larry is still as good a as fellow. (By the way, did you see Larry in *Godfather III?* He did a very nice job.)

Other family members also got involved in my life and my business. My younger brother Lester, for example, helped me build a cottage industry out of wacky promotional items.

Remember the Pride-and-Joy business card? Well that was just the beginning. Up in my apartment in New York, I've got boxes of the kind of screwball promotions that I've given away for decades.

There is, for example, a little number consisting of a dime soldered onto a safety pin. It's called a dime-and-pin, as in, "I'd like to give you this dime-and-pin." I also hand out Henny Youngman "Make No Mistake" pencils with erasers at both ends of the writing utensils.

And who could ever forget the Henny Youngman "Everyone Can Use an Extra Inch" thirteen-inch-foot ruler? Naturally, each of these items came adorned with my name, address, home phone number, and a plea for work.

The man behind these promotions was my younger brother Lester. In time he even went into business himself, producing dime-and-pins by the truckful. Lester was a good man, and I miss him every day.

Oh, to have a family such as mine working on your side! I still remember the whole *mishpocheh,* every relation from every which side of the clan, coming to see my opening night at the Copacabana not long after I'd decided my home was to be New York, not Hollywood.

Peeking through the Copa's curtains a few minutes before I was due to go on, I saw them all seated and clucking at several front tables. I tried to read their lips; I was sure I made out my mother-in-law, Mrs. Cohen, saying, "So who *knew* that that BUM could make a living from this." As they say, behind every successful man is a surprised mother-in-law.

Also sitting at one of the front tables for that opening was my once-upon-a-time boss, the famous Billy Rose. By now, Billy was an even more renowned syndicated columnist. A good review from Billy Rose would be as good a plug as from Walter Winchell in the old days.

But for me, Rose also carried the specter of doom. It wasn't anything personal; it was just that the columnist was famous for not liking comics, no matter how funny they were.

Billy Rose understood that hot comics were good business, and he always stuffed his clubs full of them. Personally, however, funny men just never seemed to make the impresario laugh or even chuckle.

So what happened on that fateful evening? Well, don't take my word for it. I still have Rose's column in which he reviewed my performance that night.

"A funnyman named Youngman," Billy Rose began, "is entertaining at the Copacabana. This patter-chatter gent has been around Broadway almost as long as the stores that sell souvenir turtles."

At this late date, I still have no idea what in the hell a souvenir turtle is. Anyway, as I read this review for the first time, I was quaking. At least Rose had the decency to admit in print that he didn't find comics particularly entertaining.

> Unfortunately, I'm not a good audience for joke tellers. And so I was a little sorry for Youngman when they planted me at a ringside table the night he opened. "At least try to look inter-

> ested," Eleanor [Holm, ex-Olympic champion and Rose's wife] said. "Henny has a wife and kids."
>
> Okay, here comes the good part.
>
> But a minute after the comic got going I found myself laughing—laughing like I haven't laughed on Broadway in a long time.

A rave from the great Billy Rose! As they say in Texas, good gravy! But the real hint of what my life would be like for the duration came in Rose's last paragraph:

"The bistro bosses around the country who are going snow blind looking at white table cloths," Rose wrote in conclusion, "could do a lot worse than hitch onto Henny."

And that's just what happened. For better or worse, in sickness and in health, for richer or poorer, I headed out on the road. My heart may have been in New York, but my body would be wherever anyone would pay me to tell jokes. It might be at the Copacabana, or it might be at a hootenanny bar mitzvah party thrown by a Billings, Montana, ranch of a cowboy named Finkelstein.

Even now, every town I play seems filled with possibility. I'm not sure what it is that caused my sometimes grievous case of wanderlust.

A big part, I think, was described in a poem by that other great artist from Brooklyn, Mr. Walt Whitman. The poem is called "I Dream'd in a Dream," and my grandson Larry brought it to my attention once when I was about to go on one more trip to someplace else.

From then on, whenever I headed out for a gig in another place I never heard of, I tried to remember Whitman's hopeful words.

"I dream'd," Walt wrote of going on the road, "that was the new city of Friends."

CHAPTER THIRTEEN

On the Road Forever, or, How I Got to Know Jack Ruby, or, Did You Hear About the Guy Who Went to Las Vegas in a $35,000 Cadillac and Came Home in a $225,000 Bus?

Whenever possible, I took Sadie and the kids with me on the road. There were times, however, when it wasn't feasible for anybody in the family to tag along. As you might imagine, traveling alone on the nightclub circuit allows one to meet quite a number of characters. Now I usually think of meeting characters as a fringe benefit of my job. Once in a while, however, it's an occupational hazard. Always, it's interesting.

In the old days, I think, the characters usually seemed *safer*. Even the scariest characters you'd meet on the circuit back then usually lived by the notion of honor among thieves. Take what happened one night years ago during my run at a Newark, New Jersey, joint called the Blue Mirror Club.

As usual, I waited around after my show that night for the Blue Mirror to close. Club owners loved it when you hung around to schmooze with departing customers; it's good PR for the place and for yourself. After waving good-bye to the last departing patrons, I gathered my coat and headed out the door.

"Hey, Henny!" my very tough-guy boss yelled, stopping me. "Where's your fiddle?"

I told the boss I'd left my violin where I always left it—in the club's locked dressing room. There was no point, I told him, in schlepping it back and forth every night I performed at the Blue Mirror.

"Go get it," he said. "You might also want to fetch any clothes you got up there."

"That's ridiculous!" I told my boss.

"Get your fiddle, Henny!" the boss bellowed with a certain malicious authority. "Okay, okay," I said as I walked to the dressing room.

That night, the Blue Mirror Club caught fire and burned to the ground. But surprise, surprise, the place was heavily insured.

As was my fiddle, in a different way. The morning after the fire, I went to view the charred remains of the Blue Mirror Club. The boss was there, smoking a cigar, looking very satisfied.

"Thanks, boss," I said.

"No problem, Henny," he said. "A man needs his fiddle." Like I said, there was honor among thieves.

In truth, the characters who often make the worst

trouble are the ones who seem as if they are the most harmless. Take this guy I got to know in Dallas named Jack Ruby.

Yes, *that* Jack Ruby. Jack, of course, owned the Carousel Club, a low-class strip joint that catered to cops, fancy hoods, show-biz people, and newspapermen. Early in life, Jack Ruby had been a street hood for the mob in Chicago. By the time I met him, Jack fancied himself a man-about-his-new-hometown of Dallas.

Jack Ruby was the kind of guy who liked to ingratiate himself with the cops, out-of-town comics, and anybody else who he thought might be semi-important. He'd always bring sandwiches and coffee to the police station houses, and buy drinks and meals for visiting entertainers during their off-hours.

He was the worst type of bully and a coward, a guy who would hit one of his strippers but would cry if somebody tough talked sideways to him. All Jack Ruby really wanted, I thought, was to be allowed to hang around, to act like a big man around the big men.

At first, I simply couldn't believe my eyes when I saw Jack Ruby shoot Lee Harvey Oswald in the basement of the Dallas jail on national television during that horrible 1963 November weekend. No, I said to Sadie, jumping out of my chair, that *couldn't* be that schlepper Jack Ruby.

But it was. And when I thought about it, it made sickening, perfect sense that Jack had done the deed. For Jack Ruby, I realized, really wanted nothing more than just to be allowed to hang around. He wanted to be a big shot himself, to have others think of him as a hero.

He'd been a lousy gangster, and a lousy operator of

a lousy strip joint. But he dreamed real big dreams that pushed him right into shooting Lee Harvey Oswald. Jack, you sonofabitch.

But for every Jack Ruby–like nut you'd run into on the road, you'd usually find a couple of gracious and sincere characters. One of my favorite such fellows was Augie Ratner, proprietor of Augie's, the classiest strip joint in the Midwest. Whenever Blaze Starr or Gypsy Rose Lee were anywhere near Minneapolis, you knew you could find them at Augie's.

Now I don't want you to think that all the people I hung around with on the road when Sadie wasn't around owned strip joints. Jack Ruby and Augie Ratner were exceptions, and they sit on opposite ends of the social spectrum. Ruby was the kind of guy you couldn't get rid of; Augie was the kind of guy you couldn't get enough of.

I remember meeting Augie one night at the Flame Room in the Radisson Hotel in Minneapolis during the war. A young woman named Norma Delores Egstrom was torch-singing that night at the Flame. I recall Miss Egstrom telling the crowd that this was the very room where she'd been discovered by Benny Goodman only a few years before.

She'd fled her parents' North Dakota farm, she said, to make it as a singer in Minneapolis. When she left town to join Benny Goodman's orchestra in Chicago, she explained, she also left behind Norma Delores Egstrom. From now on, she was Miss Peggy Lee.

Augie was most impressed with the sentimentality of Peggy Lee's return engagement to the Flame and Minneapolis. An ex-boxer, Augie wore his heart on his sleeve like so many tough guys who've been tenderized by a little age. But only a guy as tough as Augie would dare cry at Peggy Lee.

Augie was also one of the most gullible people I ever met. Hence, it's no surprise to me that one of my favorite practical jokes ever came at Augie's expense. It happened, as these things probably should, in Las Vegas. Augie was in Vegas on vacation; I was playing one of the casino showrooms.

We all know, of course, how big gamblers get complimentary food and lodging in Vegas. But in the early days of the gambling town, the hotels would also pour huge platters of free food into even their chintziest gamblers. Sit down in any Las Vegas dining room back then, and a food orgy would be forced upon you.

Now Augie was never a man to turn down a feast. In fact, it's safe to say that Augie Ratner was a *fresser,* which is Yiddish for, well, a man who never turns down a feast. Anyway, one lunchtime in Vegas, I'm watching him put it away like I've never seen before. A whole chicken. Three steaks. Five potatoes. Six eggs.

Finally, I couldn't take it anymore. I turned to Augie, and told him in a quite serious tone that if he didn't watch it, all that food was going to fatten up his head so much that his hat would no longer fit.

Hearing this, Augie harrumphed. Ignoring my warnings, he bit into a just-delivered club sandwich. At this point, I excused myself for a moment and repaired to the hotel lobby. There, I walked over to the coat check, and fished out the receipt for my jacket. It was number 210. I then gave the coat-check girl twenty bucks to lend me number 211. This number, I knew from when we came in, was Augie's beloved porkpie hat.

With Augie's hat in hand, I hightailed it over to the lobby newsstand, where I purchased a *Las Vegas Sun*. Then I crinkled a couple pages of newsprint, and tucked the paper wad inside the rim of Augie's hat. Finally, it was back to the coat check, where I returned the secretly vandalized hat.

Dear readers, I take it you can see where this practical joke is heading. Finally, Augie finishes his gluttonous performance in the Flamingo dining room. We walk out into the lobby. I get my coat, Augie gets his hat. Augie tries on said hat.

The porkpie *chapeau,* bulked up with newspaper, is now too small for Augie's head. Being the most gullible man since Chicken Little, Augie turns pale and starts shaking. "Henny, you're right!" Augie said with a shudder, his porkpie hat perched precariously on his head. "I ate so much my head got fat!"

He believed it. What can I say, but the man *actually* believed it?

The point of this is that every town on the road has its own kind of rules and magic. In his hometown of Minneapolis, you could never convince a savvy strip-joint operator like Augie Ratner that his hat no longer fits because he's just stuffed his face. But in the lobby of the Flamingo Hotel in Las Vegas, it's not so hard.

Many things about Las Vegas first became clear in that very lobby. Take the end of the reign of Bugsy Siegel, the gangster who invented Las Vegas. Bugsy's permanent retirement was actually announced right there in the Flamingo's lobby.

Bugsy, backed by the mob, had opened the Flamingo, the first modern casino, in 1946. But when the Syndicate discovered Bugsy was skimming, he was dispatched in Los Angeles with a bullet through the eye. Twenty minutes after the shooting, two gangsters named Little Moe Sedway and and Gus "Big Greenie" Greenbaum walked into the lobby of the Flamingo and announced they were taking over.

If this was how they treated the executives in old Las Vegas, you can imagine how they treated the performers. I guess it was the mid-fifties when I learned that there was indeed a different set of rules in Las Vegas.

I was taught this lesson the hard way. At the time, I was working two shows a night at the Sands. Across the street at the Frontier, meantime, schlock singer Mario Lanza was about to open a run of his own. Lanza, of course, thought of himself as Enrico Caruso by way of Elvis Presley. Those who had to deal with him professionally thought of him as a drunk who often suffered crippling attacks of stage fright.

In show-biz lingo, such attacks are called "flop sweat." And, as luck would have it, Lanza developed a monumental case of flop sweat twenty-four hours before he was to open across the street from me at the Frontier.

So what does this have to do with me? Plenty, it turned out. The night of Lanza's supposed opening, Jack Entratter, my boss at the Sands, asked me to do a favor. Would I please help the competition and fill in with Billy Eckstein across the street at the Frontier?

Sure, I said. So that night I did my two shows at the Sands and two more for Lanza at the Frontier. The crooner still had his flop sweat the next night, so I had to do another four shows at the two casinos.

The next day I asked Jack Entratter which hotel

would be paying me for the extra two shows a day I was playing. "What do you mean, *paying?*" Entratter asked, looking genuinely shocked. "In Vegas, we hotel people have a reciprocal agreement to exchange talent in case of an emergency," he explained. "See, if *you* got sick, Lanza would go on for you."

Very nice. Enraged, I lectured Entratter about an old show-biz tradition whereby if *I* play, *you* pay. I got more and more steamed as I explained the principle, and began shouting at my boss. Finally, with my voice rattling the Tiffany lamp in Jack's office, I up and quit.

My bravado stemmed mostly from the fact that the previous night I'd been offered a thousand-dollar-a-week raise to jump from the Sands to the Frontier. Sammy Lewis, the Frontier's boss, had heard me fill in for Lanza, and had told me he wanted to dump Elvis Caruso and hire me outright.

So, immediately after telling off Entratter and quitting the Sands, I crossed the street and marched into Sammy Lewis's office. Sticking out my hand for a shake, I told him I would be happy to accept his offer.

"What offer?" Sammy said.

Apparently, Sammy was having problems with his short-term memory. "Impossible," he said after I reminded him of what he'd offered me the previous night. "I couldn't have said that," he continued. "In Vegas, we hotel people have a reciprocal agreement among ourselves not to boost salaries by trying to steal acts from one another."

Ah, it had been a pleasant morning. Between all the secret agreements between casinos, I had lost two jobs. As I wandered back to my room in the Sands to pack my bags, I realized one of the fundamental truths of success in any field.

Never, and I repeat, *never,* talk business when you're angry.

And this was but my first education in the strange ways of Las Vegas. It's funny how the town has changed over the decades. In a lot of ways, it's become like any other resort town. Unlike the days of Bugsy Siegel, Vegas hotels now change hands in mergers and acquisitions, and not with bullets through the eye. Nowadays, the guys who run the casinos are trained in business school, not Murder, Inc.

Last week, someone sent me the course catalog from the University of Nevada-Las Vegas Casino Management School. Here's Hotel Administration 399, a course, I kid you not, entitled "Protection of Casino Table Games."

The class, says the catalog, provides "an in-depth examination of the various methods used to protect casino table games. The course reviews blackjack, baccarat, poker, craps, and roulette, examining possible ways that cheating can occur. Methods of detection and various internal controls used by the casino will be discussed."

My God, if classes like this had been around when I was a kid, I might have gotten a Ph.D.!

Still, despite all the changes, there are some basic and valuable lessons of casino life that live on from Vegas's Wild West days. For instance, we've got the strange, sad case of poor Donald Trump.

The smart money in Vegas and Atlantic City knew Trump was losing his grip months before the world discovered he was a virtual deadbeat. How did they know? Because of what Trump did in his casino last year as some Japanese high roller was playing baccarat for $200,000 a hand. While this Japanese guy played, you see, Trump paced nervously behind the gambler's back. Enraged, the Japanese guy stormed out of The Donald's casino.

Trump, you see, had violated the ancient Casino Commandment Number One: "Don't sweat the action."

It's a wise lesson, even if you don't own a casino. Unfortunately, I had to learn the meaning of this law the hard way. (I can just hear Sadie saying to this, "So, what else is new?")

For proof, I have the sorry spectacle I made of myself during my first appearance on *The Ed Sullivan Show.* During rehearsals, Ed couldn't stop futzing around with my material. He'd tell me to take out this joke, do that joke, on second thought put this joke back in, and so on and so forth.

This, coming from a man who was the world's most famous stiff. Ed himself knew he lacked a certain, shall we say, *warmth.* No dummy, Sullivan was always trying to cook up ways to look more likable on camera. When his show first went on the air, for example, Ed tried to make himself seem more human by having a comic heckler give him the business every week from the audience.

The person Ed picked for the part of the heckler was his old pal Patsy Flick, a woman who'd been a Yiddish dialect comic in vaudeville. Every show for that first season, Flick would give Ed the needle in her heavy accent, yelling things like "Did you look dat vay vhen you ver alive?" or "Come on, Soloman, for God's sake, smile. It makes you look sexy." Unfortunately, it didn't work. Even later, paired with Topo Gigio, Ed never came across as a man with a funny bone in his wooden-looking body.

Still, Ed Sullivan kept giving me advice and hammering away at my routine up until the very second I went on for my premiere. "Do that joke," Ed kept saying. "On second thought, don't do that joke. We'll see about doing that joke."

All during our rehearsals, I just took it. What, after all, could I say to the great Ed Sullivan? It was his candy store. So I did as I was told. Still, I couldn't help but get more and more rattled with each of Sullivan's new demands. By showtime, I was a complete wreck. My timing was off, my routine had been altered, and I couldn't find a tempo. I bombed, coast to coast.

And why? Because I sweated the action. Remember, students, unlike me and Donald Trump, *don't sweat the action.*

I know, I know, when it comes to the kind of ancient wisdom I offer, it's easier said than done. For proof of this, we have what happened backstage on the Sullivan show after I *plotst.*

I was livid that night. Ed, I thought, was responsible for the destruction of my act and my public humiliation. So what did I do? I yelled at Ed Sullivan. Let me repeat that. *I yelled at Ed Sullivan.*

Now nobody yells at Ed Sullivan, not even Elvis Presley with his wiggling hips. And certainly not Henny Youngman, with his kids needing braces and his wife who wouldn't mind a mink coat one of these years.

As I said, I yelled at Ed Sullivan. Now what was one

of those all-important commandments I'd learned in Las Vegas and lectured you about? Oh, yeah.

Never, and I repeat, *never,* talk business when you're angry.

My penalty for blowing up at Ed was a five-year banishment from Topo Gigio's Kingdom. Thankfully, I killed the audience my first show back, and Ed Sullivan treated me forever after like the returned prodigal son.

I was giddy with excitement right after my triumphant return to Sullivan Land. I still remember hurrying into the performers' dressing room after the show and grabbing my violin case. I then headed out of the studio, hailed a cab, and headed straight for Lindy's to celebrate with the boys.

The radio was on in the cab, and as we neared the restaurant, a news bulletin interrupted the music. If anybody has seen Henny Youngman, the announcer said, please have him contact the police. Youngman, the reporter continued, is believed to have violinist Isaac Stern's priceless Stradivarius in his possession.

Gulp. Isaac Stern had provided the cultural entertainment on that evening's *Ed Sullivan Show.* I looked down at the violin case next to me. No, this was definitely not my case.

I directed the cabbie to turn around. On the way, I dared to sneak a peek at the kind of instrument my parents had dreamed I'd one day play. The Stradivarius was so beautiful and delicate that it brought tears to my eyes.

I was embarrassed, Isaac Stern was relieved, and Ed Sullivan was ecstatic. You couldn't buy the press this incident brought the show. From then on, Ed Sullivan had me on his program several times a year. Once, I even asked him about our big fight years before. Ed said he didn't know what incident I was talking about.

Which only goes to show you one more commandment of show business and life:

Don't despair if you've done business in anger. In time, if you're lucky, whoever you've offended will forget what you did.

CHAPTER FOURTEEN

Back at the Friars Club, or, Take My Life, Please!

Well, I'd love to sit here all day and discuss with you, dear reader, the deep meaning of my life. I'd like to, but I can't. For after lunch here at the Friars Club, I'm leaving for the airport and an engagement in Cincinnati. After Cincy, it's on to Toledo, then I'm off to Los Angeles, where I'll be shooting an episode of Jane Curtin's new sitcom.

As it is, I'm running late. And I still haven't gotten my lunch! Perhaps you still remember Steve, my regular Friars Club waiter whom I introduced in the first chapter? Well, I still call him Statue, because that's *still* how fast he moves.

Ah, here he is. At this moment, Statue is placing in

front of me the half-grapefruit I ordered several hours ago. "Statue!" I yell at him. "I told you specifically that I wanted the *bottom* half of the grapefruit!"

Oh my, look who just walked into the dining room. It's none other than Milton Berle. Excuse me, dear readers, but Milton will be insulted if I don't insult him from across the room.

"Milton!" I yell. "You look exactly the same as you did twenty years ago. Old!"

Not that I, at eighty-six, am one to talk. But while I admit to sometimes feeling a little aged, I've never felt the least bit dated. That's because fads come and go in comedy. But the one-liner always remains sacred. People laughed at these jokes when I told them at Legs Diamond's Hotsy Totsy Club sixty years ago—and they're still laughing at these same one-liners at joints I play today.

To me, the key is to keep the joke compact. You want to make it easy for the audience to *visualize* the gag. Let me give you an example. "They're a very strange-looking couple. The wife is bowlegged, the husband is knock-kneed. When they stand together, they spell OX." *Capisce?* This a joke that jumps before your eyes and into your imagination.

Not that I'm any comedy theorist. To be honest, I've never understood all this technical talk of stuff like comic "timing." Even when masters like Groucho Marx told me to slow down in my delivery to milk the audience and save material, I refused to pay heed. Who's got time, I figured, for proper transitions and segues between jokes?

For instance, let's take a segment of my act from one of my recent performances. A friend made me a transcript of this show; since we're talking about timing, I'll start at the point in the act where I raise this very subject.

> Folks, my timing is off lately. When I sit down to eat, I get sexy. When I go to bed, I get hungry. People are crazy these days! I saw a man lying in the street. I said, "Can I help you?" He said, "No, I just found a parking space and sent my wife to buy a car." It's just murderous what's going on with people today. One fellow comes up to me on the street in New York and says he hasn't eaten in three days. I say, "Force yourself." Another guy comes up and says he hasn't eaten in a week. I say, "Don't worry, it tastes the same." All right, we're rolling! I love this crowd!

These jokes were all delivered in the time it takes brainier comics to simply clear their throats. What I'm trying to say is that even when one-liners go out of style, I know they'll soon be back.

Take the continuing popularity of Dial-a-Joke, New York Telephone's nice little racket whereby callers, for the price of one message unit, get one minute of taped one-liners. Yours truly was the original Dial-a-Joke comic, and I've never felt more popular than when I saw the sheer number of people who paid to call up my most famous one-liners.

One-liners are even popular at the times when you'd least expect it. Take the late 1960s, when every comic seemed to be doing rambling "topical" monologues. Suddenly, from out of nowhere, comes *Rowan and Martin's Laugh-In,* a prime-time television show motored entirely on one-liners. True, the jokes were all about beatniks, hepcats, and what have you. But they were one-liners.

I myself had been pitching the idea of a television show built on one-liners for years. I just *knew* it would be a smash. So I was amazed when *Laugh-In*'s producer, George Schlatter, finally convinced the network mucketymucks to give the show a shot. But I wasn't surprised when the show hit comedy pay dirt.

George, always a big fan and good friend of mine, had me on *Laugh-In* innumerable times. Now that the show is being rerun every night on cable, I'm being discovered by a whole generation that was brought up not on vaudeville and Kate Smith but on Nintendo and microwave popcorn.

A few years back, George Schlatter also paid me a heartfelt, if slightly strange, compliment. A mutual friend of ours in the comedy business had just died, and George had an idea of how to send him out in proper one-liner style.

At the time, I had a little plastic gizmo in the shape of my face out on the market. When you pushed the plastic *shnoz,* the battery-powered device uttered one of my one-liners. With terrific toys like this around back then, who the hell needed Nintendo?

Anyway, George has the idea of placing the joke machine in the open casket of our friend. His thought was to have each mourner press the *shnoz* as he came up to pay his final respects. George checked with the widow, who said it was exactly the kind of send-off our friend would want.

Funeral day arrives, and George is the first down to

say good-bye to our pal. After pausing in meditation, he reaches into the casket and presses the *shnoz* of the joke machine. The first joke out, no kidding, was, "My doctor gave me six months to live. But I couldn't pay the bill, so he gave me another six months."

The funeral party paused, then laughed, then laughed for real. From then on, each mourner pressed the joke nose as he prayed at the bier. At first it was disconcerting seeing people laughing at a funeral. But as I watched from the back pew, I thought to myself that maybe this was the meaning of going in style. Always leave 'em laughing, doncha know.

However, such morbid thoughts evaporated as soon as I hit the sunshine outside the funeral home. I figured I didn't have time to worry about such things.

Even now, at eighty-six, I know that you're never too old to play another gig. You're never too old to appear in another movie or make another commercial. And you're *certainly* never too old to work the phone and drum up business.

You're even never too old to become a Man.

Hmm. Sounds heavy, huh, downright philosophical? Actually, I'm just speaking the literal truth. Remember way back in this book when I described how I lost my bar mitzvah because of the sudden death of my Uncle Velvl?

Well, about a dozen years ago, I mentioned my bar mitzvahlessness to *Y*, the head of *Y* resort. I'd always been mildly embarrassed about this fact, but *Y* expressed complete astonishment. Suddenly, a light bulb went on over his head.

"Henny," he said, "we're going to give you the bar mitzvah you never had! A big one, a real one, right here at the resort."

And so he did, right in the resort's ballroom-cum-synagogue. It was a bar mitzvah with all the trimmings —trimmings I would never have had if my original date sixty years before had gone on as scheduled.

However, the most important thing about retrieving my long-lost bar mitzvah wasn't the food and party. No, the part I liked best was that I was finally able to publicly say those classic words usually uttered by thirteen-year-old boys with peach fuzz and braces.

"Today," I announced to the world at seventy-three, "I am a Man."

So you see, I wasn't speaking as a philosopher, but as just plain me, when I say you're never too old to become a Man.

Excuse me, dear readers, I'm a little thirsty. I think I'll have to put my friend Steve the Friars Club waiter back to work. "Hey, Statue! Have you got a little orange juice you're not using? And by the way, is your family happy? Or do you come home at night?"

Sorry about the interruption. Anyway, it's never been a problem finding the motivation to get on another plane, in order to go on another stage in order to tell another joke. Actually, I'm lying. There was such a time, and it was only a few years ago.

My beloved Sadie, my million-dollar baby (before taxes), was dying of cancer. She was a trouper, without ever a complaint about her lot. Instead, she reassured and comforted *me*. I still remember staying up late with Sadie one night shortly before the end.

Sadie knew I was having trouble telling the wife jokes in my act while she was sick. Even though Sadie and I had lived and built a family on those wife jokes, it no longer seemed right for me to be making that kind of joke while Sadie was at home fighting for her life.

When I told her this, Sadie harrumphed louder than I'd heard her harrumph since 1947. "Henny," she said, "tell the jokes. And after I'm gone, *keep* telling them."

And so I have.

In his will, Jack Benny made a provision for his wife, Mary, to be sent a perfect red rose every day after he died. Likewise, Sadie's posthumous gift to me was those one-liners. And every time I tell one of my wife jokes, I remember how much I love her. Because it's not really Sadie that I'm talking about when I tell my audiences things like:

> My wife will buy anything marked down. Yesterday she brought home two dresses and an escalator.

Or:

> I've been married for fifty years and I'm still in love with the same woman. If my wife ever finds out, she'll kill me.

Or:

> My wife was at the beauty shop for two hours, and that was just for the estimate.

Still, some may wonder, how can I possibly express my love for Sadie by telling jokes like these? I have no answer. All I know is that Sadie herself laughed at the jokes. And she didn't seem to object to the life we were able to build on the strength of jokes that ostensibly made fun of her and her mother. She never once took it seriously when I told an audience:

> Some people ask the secret of Sadie's and my long marriage. The secret is that we take time to go to a romantic restaurant two times a week. A little candlelight, dinner, soft music and dancing. She goes Tuesdays; I go Fridays.

Despite Sadie ordering me to keep doing these jokes, I just didn't have the heart to tell them after she died. Life just wasn't the same if I could no longer call Sadie immediately after each and every show to tell her how I'd done and what the crowd was like.

But I'm a pro. Which, after being a good husband, father, and grandfather, is the thing I'm most proud of in my life. So I always went on. And, in time, my heart came back to my performance. I felt Sadie was *with* me onstage, and that she was still laughing at every single one of my wife jokes.

I know it sounds clichéd, but the audience has become my reason to keep going. Now more than ever, after sixty-plus years onstage, I never feel so young, so alive, so happy, as when I'm making the people laugh.

I'm not embarrassed by this fact. Indeed, I now finish each of my performances by singing a little ditty that is part confessional, part thank-you to all the people who have come to see me over the years. The song's called "All I Want Is an Audience," and goes, a cappella, something like this:

All I want is an audience,
An audience like you
I want to hear you laugh and applaud the thing I do
Go on and call me a ham
I don't give a damn;
I'm confessing that it's true
All I want is an audience
With an audience, like *you*.

I've had many *new* audiences since Sadie passed on. For this, I mostly have to thank Lee Salomon, the hottest agent in all of agenting. Still, I guess my favorite new audience was the entire city of San Francisco. It happened because my good friend Eddie Spizel, probably San Francisco's best advertising man, came up with a campaign not long ago for the Bay Area Rapid Transit company featuring me. The tag line for each of the television commercials was "Take My BART. Please!" Ridership skyrocketed, and I had the pleasure of knowing that my work was environmentally correct.

Of course, some of my very *best* audiences can be found each lunchtime right here in the dining room of the Friars Club. As I've mentioned, this is where a lot of successful kid comics come each day looking for blessings and show-biz wisdom from us old guys.

Sometimes, if the kid comics are fresh or a little cocky, I just give them bullshit stories until Statue arrives with my soup. "Say," I'll say to these youngsters, "let me tell you about the time I went miniature golfing a hundred years ago with Irving Thalberg and Fanny Brice." Or was that pinochle with Meyer Lansky and Gloria Swanson? Who the hell knows.

But if these comics are nice kids like Robin Williams or Billy Crystal or Jay Leno, I give them the real goods. I give them the few nuggets of wisdom I've accumulated over my generations on the stage. You, dear reader, have seen these few nuggets sprinkled throughout this book. But since I myself can never remember much the first time around, I thought I'd summarize what I've laid out for you so far. For more in-depth explanations, you're just going to have to read this book all over again. Okay. Here it is:

Youngman's Laws of Show Biz and Life

I. *Nem di Gelt.* Take the money. Don't believe what people tell you about what they're going to do for you tomorrow—*nem di Gelt.* Similarly, don't price yourself out of the market. Swallow your pride. *Nem di Gelt.*

II. Stay on phones. Let 'em know you're alive.

III. Don't do business while you're angry. Trust me.

IV. If you make a mistake and do business while you're angry, don't despair. Maybe they'll forget.

V. Don't sweat the action. Remember Donald Trump behind the baccarat table.

VI. Remember the old phrase *Mensh tracht, Gott lacht.* It literally means, "Man plans, God laughs." It really means, "Don't plot your life—*live* it."

VII. Finally, and most important, fall in love. And stay in love.

Most of these kid comics, however, don't want to hear it. And who can blame them? Why, a few even try to educate *me*!

Take this hip comic who specializes in topical humor who approached my table at the Friars Club two days ago. (You want topical humor? Here: "I knew the Savings and Loan industry was in trouble when my banker knocked on my door and asked for his calendar back.")

Anyway, Mr. Newspaper Headline came near and gave me this tape of Andrew Dice Clay, this hotshot kid comic from Brooklyn with the filthy mouth. "Go home and listen," the comic told me. "This is what's hot right now."

When I got home, I plugged in the tape. After listening to a few gags, I realized that Andrew Dice Clay needs no introduction. What he needs is an act.

He also needs some unasked-for career advice from one who knows. Me.

For starters, it's not that the words Andrew Dice Clay uses shock me. Fifty years ago, when I myself was a hotshot kid comic from Brooklyn, I heard those same words come out of Dodger manager Leo Durocher every time the Giants came to Ebbets Field. The difference between Leo the Lip and Andrew Dice Clay is that Leo was funny.

It reminds me of the guy who went to a psychiatrist. The psychiatrist tells him, "You're crazy." The guy says, "I want a second opinion." The psychiatrist says, "Okay. You're ugly too."

Well, Andrew Dice Clay, you remind me of that guy. You're crazy if you think poking fun at the helpless people makes you a comedian. My second opinion is that your jokes aren't jokes, they're ugliness.

So who am I to come off as Rabbi Pious I? Granted, I'm no deep thinker. About as heavy as I get in my act is: "God sneezed. What could I say to Him?" Still, at eighty-six, I still consider myself fairly righteous. For over sixty years, I've worked a clean act. I don't drink, smoke, or chase women. In fact, Lloyd's of London once gave 6 to 1 that I was dead.

Still, this doesn't stop the parade of young comics to my table in the Friars Club. Lasting, lasting, they all want to know the secret to lasting.

If you're good, I tell each of these kids, you'll last. You'll have your high times and your low times, but you'll last. And how can you tell if you've been so blessed? Who knows? What's easier to predict is a flash in the pan.

Like Andrew Dice Clay, Sam Kinison, or any of those other so-called comedians who spout only meanness and hate. It was just a couple of days ago that I saw Clay was going to be on the *Arsenio Hall Show*. Figuring he'd have to clean up his act for TV, I gave him another chance.

When I tuned in, however, I saw a man who couldn't adlib an argument without a TelePrompter. Instead of telling jokes, he told everybody how nobody understands him, how he's a sensitive artist. I kid you not, he almost started crying. What could Arsenio do, but treat him like Milton Berle? Berle, of course, was a TV pioneer: He was the first to be turned off.

So Andrew and your ilk, do us a favor. Be a mensh. Tell jokes. If you've got to go ethnic, take out the hate and bring us together. Impossible, you say? Didn't you hear about the American Indian girl who married a Jewish boy? They decided to give their new son a name to please both sides of the family. They named him Whitefish.

Finally, Andrew, stop complaining about your difficult life. The next time you go on Johnny or Arsenio, don't tell us how you became a comic because your mother conflicted you as a kid. No one wants to know from you and your mother. It's not funny.

Your mother-in-law, of course, is another story.

Index

INDEX

INDEX

INDEX

INDEX

INDEX

INDEX

INDEX